Contemplation

by

Francis Kelly Nemeck, O.M.I.
and Marie Theresa Coombs, Hermit

A Michael Glazier Book
THE LITURGICAL PRESS
Collegeville, Minnesota

ACKNOWLEDGEMENTS

We gratefully acknowledge those hundreds of persons who have passed through Lebh Shomea House of Prayer. Their search, their questions and their challenges have helped make us aware of the need to compose this book and to express more accurately the truths herein contained.

6	7	8	9

Library of Congress Cataloging-in-Publication Data

Nemeck Francis Kelly, 1936-
    Contemplation / by Francis Kelly Nemeck and Marie Theresa Coombs.
       p.   cm.
    "A Michael Glazier book."
    Reprint. Originally published: Wilmington, Del. : M. Glazier,
1982.
    ISBN 0-8146-5283-2
    1. Contemplation. 2. Prayer—Catholic Church. 3. Catholic
Church—Doctrines. I. Coombs, Marie Theresa. II. Title.
III. Series.
BV5091.C7N45 1990
    248.3'4—dc20
                            90-43534
                                CIP

Table of Contents

To Christ Jesus
Yesterday—Today—Forever

Principal Abbreviations and General Notes

Ascent   St. John of the Cross, *The Ascent of Mount Carmel.*

Canticle St. John of the Cross, *The Spiritual Canticle* (2nd redaction).

Cloud   *The Cloud of Unknowing* (various translations).

CP   Thomas Merton, *Contemplative Prayer* (Image D285, 1971).

DM   Pierre Teilhard de Chardin, *The Divine Milieu* (Harper, TB 384G, 1965).

Flame   St. John of the Cross, *The Living Flame of Love* (2nd redaction).

Night   St. John of the Cross, *The Dark Night of the Soul.*

PC   William Johnston, trans., *The Book of Privy Counseling* (by the author of the *Cloud*).

TS   Thomas Merton, *Thoughts in Solitude* (Image D247, 1968).

Note 1. All translations from Hebrew, Greek, Latin, French and Spanish sources are our own.

Note 2. References to the Bible and to classical spiritual authors are made in the usual manner.

Note 3. The psychology and anthropology which underlie our presentation may in places reflect terminology that appears neo-scholastic in tone. However, let the reader not apply too hastily the categories of the schoolmen to our mode of expression. For example, we use the word "soul" throughout this study not so much in the Thomistic sense of the *corpus-anima* distinction, but rather in the traditional mystical sense derived from the New Testament *psyche* and the Hebrew *nephesh*: namely, the deepest and most mysterious aspects of the human person being acted upon directly by God.

Introduction

Since Vatican II, in western Christendom at least, the term "contemplation" has become something of a household word. In the long run, this fact will probably turn out to be more beneficial for the development of spirituality than the extremely restricted usage of the term prior to the Council. However, too popular a usage of any expression tends to take away from its deep inner significance. Thus the importance of this present book: to re-present the deepest insights of the western Christian tradition regarding the mystery of contemplation.

This study is not presented in the form of an historical development (although a great deal of historical development is presupposed). Rather it is presented in the manner of a pastorally oriented theological synthesis. *It is a theological and pastoral reflection on certain aspects of the mystery of contemplation according to the principles of St. John of the Cross, for those who experience an ever increasing need to allow God to permeate more and more their entire being.*

With so many books on the market today about contemplative prayer — some of which are quite worthwhile — why add another? The basic response to this question is that aside from certain classical spiritual masters — the author of the *Cloud*, St. John of the Cross, Thomas Merton, for example — we know of no writers who specifically address themselves in sufficient length and depth to the very difficult and crucial question: What is contemplation in itself? And even more particularly, what is contemplation at its inception within the soul?   *a call to be a contemplat*

The beginning of contemplation is indeed a most difficult and crucial threshold in the process of transformation. We say "most difficult and crucial" both for the soul undergoing God as well as for the spiritual director trying to guide the soul through the intricacies of discernment which such a threshold necessarily entails.

Almost inevitably, when God begins to lead the soul along the way of contemplation — which in fact is not a "way" at all[1] — the soul becomes quite normally confused and anxious, fearing that it is slipping away from God. What is actually progress in holiness often appears as regression into self.

This present study then is a careful reflection upon God's activity within the soul as well as the soul's struggling response

---

[1] "On this road" to transforming union, "to lose one's way is to enter upon the road" of contemplation. "In other words, to pass on to the goal and leave one's way is to enter upon that which has no way at all: which is God. For the soul that arrives at this state no longer has any ways or methods of its own . . . though it does have within itself all ways, like one who possesses nothing, yet possesses all things" (*Ascent*, II, 4, 5). See CP, pp. 92-93.

to his transforming love. We will examine particularly the subtle, obscure beginning of contemplation, focusing especially on its nature, on the soul's growing awareness of it, on the basic principles for discerning its authenticity, as well as on certain difficulties (and other effects) arising from the experience of contemplative prayer.

Hopefully, therefore, this work will assist those whom God is calling to a more conscious and voluntary response to his initiative by offering them a deeper understanding of the mystery which is transpiring within them.

The reader will notice that certain sections of this study are somewhat technical. The reason for this is twofold. On the one hand, we are presenting a theological synthesis (not merely a summary or a popularization). Thus, we believe that it is important to furnish the serious reader with data which substantiates the theological options that we have taken. On the other hand, the technical apparatus offers avenues of further research into specific questions which spiritual directors in particular may want or need to pursue.

In any case, we urge that this work be studied (not just "read") in a slow, leisurely manner and with a "listening heart" (1 K 3:9). And since the subject being treated is living mystery, one should not be surprised to find that we do "teach spiritual things spiritually" (1 Co 2:13): that is, not clearly and precisely, not in a tangible and "sure" way, not even deductively and logically, but rather mysteriously, gropingly, as in a "dark night."

Thus, as you proceed, you will gradually discover that the initial chapters are appreciated better in the light of the latter ones. Then, having studied this work all the way through, if *read it twice*

Beloved !!

you re-study the whole a second time, the truth herein presented will be perceived even more profoundly. Finally, if you prayerfully study this treatise five or ten years hence, you will come to a still greater awareness of the mystery of transforming love within yourself.

Among St. Paul's final words to the Corinthians we find this challenge: "Examine yourselves to make sure that you are in the faith: test yourselves" (2 Co 13:5). What Paul means by "in the faith" he explains in the form of a single question which he expects every true Christian to be able to answer in all candor: "Do you acknowledge that Jesus Christ is really in you? If not, you have failed the test" (2 Co 13:5).

Well, then, do *you* acknowledge that Jesus Christ is really in you? Do you personally experience the fact that he is truly living and loving within your innermost being? Can you actually say: "I live now no longer I, but Christ lives in me" (Ga 2:20)? If not, you may be failing "the test."

This present study has been prepared to help you "examine yourself" so that you can in fact respond more consciously and lovingly to God's transforming love within you.

1

The Universal Call
to Holiness

Scripture and Tradition emphatically affirm the universality of the call to holiness: "Jesus . . . preached holiness of life to each and every one of his disciples regardless of their state in life: 'Be perfect, as your heavenly Father is perfect' (Mt 5:48)"[1]

To explore the relationship between contemplation and the universal call to holiness, we address three aspects of the mystery: (A) holiness as an attribute of God, (B) our call to holiness, and (C) our response to the universal call to holiness.

---

[1] *Dogmatic Constitution on the Church*, n. 40. No doubt, Jesus is referring to Lv 19:2: "Be holy, for I, Yahweh your God, am holy." See 1 P 1:15-16.

A. God as Holy

God's revelation of himself as holy and the awakening consciousness of his people to the full import of this truth has a long and varied history.

In Scripture itself, the development of this revelation can be traced from Moses, through the judges, kings and prophets up to the New Testament where it reaches its apex in Christ: "the Holy One of God" (Mk 1:24). Jesus in turn speaks of the "Holy Father" (Jn 17:11) and of the "Holy Spirit" (Mk 13:11).

What does it mean "to be holy"?

Etymologically, our term "holy" derives from the Anglo-Saxon *hal* meaning "whole" or "well." The word "holy" is the usual English translation for the Greek New Testament *hagios*, which in turn renders the Hebrew root *q-d-sh*. *Qadash* (verb), *qodesh* (noun), *qadosh* (adjective) all denote that which is separated from the common and the ordinary.

Applied to God and his cult, *qadash* (verb) signifies: "to be holy, to consecrate" (in the Qal stem); "to be sanctified, to be reverenced" (in the Niphal); "to set apart for sacred use, to keep holy" (in the Piel); "to be regarded as sacred, consecrated" (in the Pual); "to prepare oneself before approaching the sacred" (in the Hithpael); and "to make holy" (in the Hiphil stem).

Qadosh (adjective) not only stresses the utter transcendence of God — the wholly Other — but also uniquely expresses his immanence: the loving, personal, intimate God.

As a divine attribute, the holiness of God *is* his divinity.

Qodesh (noun) denotes that which in his being is most mysterious, most ineffable. It denotes that which constitutes God as God. Holiness is the very essence of Yahweh who so transcends the perceptible that when he does manifest himself, what is actually perceived is not God's holiness as such, but rather his glory (*kabod*).

Yet he who is wholly Other is also wholly immanent (Dt 4:7, 34, 37). Yahweh is forever the intimate lover of his people, a people he espoused to himself uniquely out of the superabundance of his love: "If Yahweh has set his heart on you and has chosen you, it was not because you were the greatest of peoples . . . it was for love of you" (Dt 7:7-8; Ho 2:21-22; 6:1-6).

Thus, the term "holiness" as applied to God denotes his innermost, secret essence, his mysterious, ineffable being which is totally distinct and separate from creation. It connotes also his incomprehensible, enduring love for his people. For the transcendence of God is historically immanent. God's holiness is at the same time both utterly transcendent and lovingly immanent.

The harmonization of these two extremes in God is unique to Judaeo-Christian revelation. This inscrutable harmony reaches its most perfect actualization in the person of Jesus, "the Word become flesh" (Jn 1:14). And it attains its most succinct expression in the theology of the beloved disciple: "God is Spirit . . . God is love." (Jn 4:24; 1 Jn 4:16).

The holiness of God in Jesus and through the Spirit produces two mysterious effects in the soul: (1) it "transforms" the human person "into the likeness" of Christ (2 Co 3:18) and (2) it wrenches forth from the human heart the

anguished experience of "dread,"[2] of "night,"[3] of utter sinfulness: "What a wretch I am, I am lost!" (Is 6:5); "What a
wretched man I am! Who will deliver me?" (Rm 7:24).

Thus, God's holiness has a twofold concomitant effect
within the soul: re-creation and purgation, sanctification and
purification — in one word: spiritualization.[4]

B. Our Call to Holiness

Flowing from these scriptural insights are two basic principles: (1) Our call to holiness is the invitation to an enduring,
personal encounter with God in himself, and as a direct
consequence of this, (2) we are gradually transformed into his
likeness and are progressively purified of all that is un-God-
like in us.

Since God alone is the source of all holiness, the one and
same holiness to which all are called irrespective of their duties
of life is an actual participation in his holiness. It is a true
participation in his very being. This participation is pure gift. It
is bestowed not because we merit him or have attained him by
our own efforts, but solely out of the superabundance of his
love.

[2]See CP, pp. 96-111.

[3]See *Night*, II, 5, 1; II, 9, 1.

[4]*Pneumatikos* is particularly a Pauline term which literally means
"spirified" or "made spiritual." It connotes the progressive passive: "having become spiritual." Of special note is Paul's use of *pneumatikos* to
designate the transformed nature of the resurrected person in 1 Co
15:44-46.

√ Love by its very nature effects union. But when God loves, the union produced by his love is *transforming* union: "Oh night which united lover with Beloved, lover transformed in the Beloved."[5]

The verb "to transform" is used four times in the New Testament: twice in transfiguration narratives (Mt 17:2; Mk 9:2) and twice by St. Paul: "Be transformed by the renewing of your mind" (Rm 12:2); "We all . . . are being transformed into the same image," that "of the Lord" (2 Co 3:18). All four instances are expressed in the passive voice, stressing the receptivity of the soul undergoing the force of divine love within it.

St. John of the Cross quite effectively synthesizes his theology of transforming union in these words: "To love is to work for God at being stripped of all that is not God. The soul then remains illuminated and transformed in God." In fact, "God so communicates his supernatural being to it that the soul seems to be God himself, possessing whatever God himself has." Moreover, "so perfect is this union that all the things both of God and of the soul are one in participant transformation." Thus, "the soul seems more God than soul. Indeed it is God by participation."[6] Yet the soul always remains truly distinct from God. Actually it reaches the pinnacle of its personal individuation in this transformation.

To put this truth in other words, the inscrutable love of God produces two interacting effects within the soul: (1)

[5] *Amada en el Amado transformada*, poem *Night*, stanza 5.

[6] *El alma más parece Dios que alma, y aun es Dios por participación*, Ascent, II, 5, 7. See PC, 13.

Transforming it in himself by participation, God (2) purges the soul of the slightest vestige of immaturity. So perfect is this loving union that the soul can be said "to have become God" — "deified," "divinized"[7] — "by participant transformation," yet always in such a way as to enhance the soul's individuality and to achieve the maximum potential of its personality.

This theology explicates the insight of St. Paul grappling with the mystery of the resurrection: "That God may be all in all" (1 Co 15:28), and that Christ may "fill all in all" (Ep 1:23).

The process of transforming-purging love begins with the act of individual existence and reaches its apex in one's personal death-resurrection: "Though this outer man of ours is falling into decay, the inner person is renewed day by day" (2 Co 4:16).

In common parlance this process is termed "call to holiness," or simply "sanctification."

C. Our Response to the Call to Holiness

Since our call to holiness is God's gift of participation in his divine life, our response must be one of loving receptivity. We become holy by letting his will be done, both directly within

---

[7]These terms go back to the very beginning of patristic mystical theology: *theosis-theoun* ("divinization," "to divinize") is found in Gregory Nazianzen and especially in Pseudo-Dionysius. *Theopoiesis-theopoiein* (deification," "to deify") is the expression used by Clement of Alexandria, Origen, Hippolytus, Basil and Athanasius.

us and through the activity we exert towards the building up of his Kingdom. Moreover, our very ability to remain lovingly receptive to him is itself gift. When God first began to create us by his love and make his home within us, he implanted this contemplative thrust deep within the inner dynamism of our life.

Progress in holiness, then, is characterized by an intensification of our receptive stance before God. "Night and day, while he sleeps and when he is awake, the seed is sprouting and growing. How? He does not know" (Mk 4:27).

God himself nurtures our growth in receptivity gradually and mysteriously, often for a long time even without our being aware of the fact. In each individual this seed of receptivity sprouts and grows in a uniquely personalized manner. Its emergence is specifically tailored by God to our individual personality and vocation. He uses all the particular events, circumstances and persons that affect us in any way as instruments through which to quicken our contemplative orientation to life.

The genesis[8] of our personal holiness attains a most critical threshold with the beginning of contemplation wherein the very nature of our personal encounter with God is transformed. Our loving receptivity, having passed through the growth process of being "first the shoot, then the ear, then the full grain in the ear" (Mk 4:27-28), is now ready for harvest. Instead of God communing with us principally through the

---

[8]We use the word "genesis" here, and throughout this study, in the technical sense employed by P. Teilhard de Chardin: "Genesis is more than simple development. It is evolution directed to a point of ultimate consummation" (Letter to T.V. Fleming, May 18, 1954).

mediation of images, objects, emotions as he had previously done in discursive meditation, he now communicates himself directly to the soul in contemplation. God's transforming and consuming love thus becomes ever more operative in this *immediate* encounter. This more interiorized phase of transformation is accompanied by a radical intensification — directly by God himself — of the soul's own loving receptivity towards him as he is in himself. This affects not only prayer, but attains every aspect of life.

With the beginning of contemplation God thrusts us headlong into a world of mystery. Here we must quite literally let go all ways to follow in the darkness of faith Christ who alone is the "Way" (Jn 14:6). From here on, progress in holiness consists in *willingly* letting God immerse us into ever more mysterious depths of personal encounter with him, and in our undergoing its consequent transforming and consuming effects, until we come to the perfect contemplation of God "face to face" (1 Co 13:12).

Integral to the universal call to holiness then is the call of every person to contemplation, at least in death. Contemplation is not reserved solely for those few called to the "contemplative life," nor is it apart from the usual process whereby God makes each of us holy. Always remaining God's free gift, contemplation is nevertheless the "ordinary" outcome of a full life of grace. "Contemplation is the summit of the Christian life of prayer"[9] — for every Christian!

---

[9]*CP*, p. 93. See *Cloud*, 34; *PC*, 11.

2

The Spirit of Prayer

An inescapable characteristic of the human spirit is its persistent restlessness, its insatiable searching: "You have made us for yourself alone, O Lord, and our heart is restless until it rests in you."[1] Complete personal fulfillment can be attained only in consummate loving union with God in himself.

This restlessness initially manifests itself to our consciousness in an obscure pull towards something more in life —something more than what actually is: something beyond the status quo. Upon deeper examination, however, we discover that this quest is not actually a desire for some-*thing* at all. It is rather the manifestation of a mysterious yearning for some-*One*, for Him-Who-Is. This "something more" which irresistibly draws us is ultimately the fullness of transformation in Christ: Our "innermost being is consumed with longing" for God (Jb 19:27).

[1] Augustine, *Confessions*, I, 1.

Our first impression is often that this searching is something of our own — something that we somehow initiate and pursue of ourselves. But in truth this insatiable yearning is a response to God who has first chosen us and who has first made his home in us (Jn 15:4, 16). We are drawn irresistibly to him solely because he has first sought us out in a most personal and intimate love. "This is the love I mean: not our love for God, but God's love for us . . . because he loved us first" (1 Jn 4:10,19).

One of the areas where this restlessness becomes manifest is in the desire for deeper personal prayer — indeed, for a *prayer-life*.

Much light has been shed on various forms of prayer: meditation, charismatic prayer, Oriental prayer attitudes, the Jesus Prayer, Prayer of the Heart, contemplative prayer, etc. Each of these approaches to praying has its own distinguishing characteristics. For example, meditation employs extensively the imagination, intellect, emotions in discoursing about God; whereas Prayer of the Heart stresses non-verbal, affective communion with God abiding in the depths of one's being.

Yet, underlying all forms of authentic prayer is a loving encounter with God in faith. All prayer — indeed life itself —necessarily tends towards loving communion with Father, Son and Spirit. No matter how much we know *about* God: his goodness, his forgiveness, his mercy, his justice, we experience him directly and immediately only in love. The real God infinitely transcends all activity, all manner of representation, all feeling. God communes most intimately with us by love, and it is in love that we most truly commune with him. Praying is ultimately "remaining loving one's Beloved."[2]

This accent on love does not exclude the use of the intellect, symbols or emotions in prayer. But such activity is nevertheless epitomized and transcended in the utter simplicity and intimacy of direct love.

Prayer is the opening up of one's deepest self to God abiding in the core of one's being. This divine indwelling is the Father generating the Son, and the Father and the Son spirating the Holy Spirit within us in space and in time. Our response then is that of loving receptivity to becoming "regenerated,"[3] loving openness to becoming "spiritual."[4]

Even in the initial phases of prayer, in which external and internal activity can be of great importance, what ultimately constitutes any way of praying as prayer is the fact that all one's activity is meant simply to open all the depths of one's being to God: "To meditate is to think. And yet successful meditation is much more than reasoning or thinking. It is much more than 'affections', much more than a series of prepared 'acts' which one goes through . . . . In meditative prayer, one thinks and speaks not only with his mind and lips, but in a certain sense with his whole being. Prayer is then not just a formula of words or a series of desires springing up in the heart — it is the orientation of our whole body, mind and spirit to God in silence, attention and adoration. All good meditative prayer is a conversion of our entire self to God."[5]

[2]*Estarse amando al Amado* (John of the Cross, *Sum of Perfection*, 4).

[3]"Unless a man be born again . . ." (Jn 3:3-8).

[4]See Rm. 8:1-27; 1 Co 15:35-38.

[5]*TS*, p. 48. See *CP*, pp. 103-104.

Since prayer is essentially a loving communion between the soul and the Trinity, "praying" is far more than simply "saying prayers." Formal prayers, novenas, litanies, Stations of the Cross as well as our personal spontaneous prayers in many instances may be permeated by a true spirit of prayer, but not automatically so. It is sometimes assumed that saying prayers is proof that one possesses a vigorous prayer life. In reality, however, the compulsive, continuous repetition of such prayers may be no more than an attempt to maintain a defensive control over one's life — a control which seemingly enables the soul to evade the *nada* that in-depth prayer necessarily entails. To cling to saying prayers, when one is actually being called to deeper prayer, does not facilitate receptivity to God. Rather, this clinging serves only to impede his transforming activity within the soul. The disinclination towards multiplicity of prayers, together with the loss of meaningfulness in discursiveness of any kind,[6] may in fact indicate progress in prayer, provided that other signs are also present.

It is especially in prayer that the living word of God "cuts like a two-edged sword, but more finely" and "slips through the place where the soul is divided from the spirit, or the joints from the marrow," judging even our most "secret thoughts" (Hb 4:12). It is particularly in prayer that the soul searching deeply for God must undergo intense storms and persevere in being led along solitary and obscure ways. It is above all in prayer that we are given the strength to resolutely pass

[6]John of the Cross uses the term "discursive" to indicate the whole gamut of internal and external activity in praying. This would include examination of conscience, both particular and general, the Rosary, the use of biblical passages in meditation, etc.

through the trials, the dread, the inner poverty that is our lot this side of the resurrection: "For though wisdom takes him at first through winding ways bringing fear and faintness on him, plaguing him with her discipline until she can trust him, and testing him with her ordeals, in the end she will lead him back to the straight road and reveal her secrets to him" (Si 4:17-18).

Thus, it is by prayer that we enter into a more quickened consciousness of the reality of death and resurrection, of night and transformation.

Authentic prayer is often experienced as a wrestling with God as well as with self. Transforming communion with God is fraught with tension. Besides our deepest desire for God, there is also present within us formidable self-centeredness, drawing us to close in upon ourselves. At one and the same time, we experience both our self struggling together with God against sin in us and our self struggling against his transforming love. We simultaneously both crave God and resist him.[7]

Yet, however effective our resistance may seem, it is inevitably God's persistent love that prevails. We cannot but end up like Jacob who finally adored the very One he had wrestled with (Gn 32:26-30); or like Jeremiah who in utter exhaustion abandoned himself to the very One he could not successfully resist (Jr 1:4-10; 20:7-9).

Our poverty is indeed so destitute that we cannot thwart indefinitely God's faithful love in our regard: "Yes, as the rain

[7]Review St. Paul's confession of his own personal interior struggle (Rm 7:14-25) and his presentation of the cosmic struggle in which we all participate (Rm 8:18-39). Paul consistently describes the soul's experience of Christ in words permeated with tension and trauma (see e.g., Ph 3:5-16; 2 Co 12:7-10).

and the snow come down from the heavens and do not return without watering the earth, making it yield and giving growth ...so the word that goes forth from my mouth" — it is Yahweh who speaks   "does not return to me empty, without carrying out my will and succeeding in what it was sent to do" (Is 55:10-11).

3

Progress in Prayer

In the Gospel we find frequent reference to the centrality of prayer in the life of Jesus. "He would always go off to some place where he could be alone and pray" (Lk 5:16). And Luke does stress *always*, not just once in a while — he was forever doing this . . . For example, before the choice of the Twelve, Jesus "spent the whole night in prayer with God" (Lk 6:12). On the morning following the cure of Simon's mother-in-law, "long before dawn, he arose, left the house, and went off to a solitary place to pray" (Mk 1:35). At the beginning of his public ministry, "Jesus was led by the Spirit out into the wilderness" (Mt 4:1).

We see Jesus at prayer on the Mount of the Transfiguration, in the garden of Gethsemane, on Calvary. Jesus not only sought out physical solitude — an actual place where he could be alone and pray. He especially lived in abiding interior solitude. That is, his humanity was always hypostatically communing with his divinity. His Person was in continuous communion with the Father: "I am in the Father and the Father is in me" (Jn 14:11); "The Father and I are one" (Jn 10:30).

Besides solitary prayer being an essential aspect of his journey to the Father, Jesus on many occasions proclaimed to his disciples the utter importance of personal prayer in their lives: "Stay awake, praying at all times" (Lk 21:36) . . . "This is the kind of spirit that can only be driven out by prayer" (Mk 9:29) . . . "Ask, and it will be given to you; seek, and you will find; knock, and the door will be opened to you" (Mt 7:7) . . . "You must come away to some desert place all by yourselves and rest awhile" (Mk 6:31) . . . "Remain in me, as I remain in you" (Jn 15:4).

Impressed by the faithfulness of Jesus to prayer and having experienced their personal need to pray, the disciples were inevitably confronted with the question of "how to pray."

On at least one occasion, a group of disciples sought direction in prayer from Jesus: "He was in a certain place praying, and when he finished one of his disciples said, 'Lord, teach us to pray, as John taught his disciples' " (Lk 11:1).

Luke presents Jesus as being in a "certain place," probably a frequented spot, a short distance from where a small group of disciples were gathered. Somehow they formed the impression that he was at prayer. After a certain lapse of time, Jesus rejoined the group. It was then that one of the neophytes posed a specific question: "John the Baptizer taught his disciples to pray. How then should we pray, Lord?"

To the Jews at that time, a particular custom or formula of prayer expressed the unique relationship with God which bound the individuals of a group together. Thus the request in Lk 11:1 shows that the followers of Jesus already recognized themselves as a primitive community. They wanted "a prayer" which would bind them together and identify them as true disciples, thereby bringing to expression the fundamental tenets of their belief in Jesus. Once the Our Father was proclaimed, prayer in Jesus's name began.

The phraseology and structure of the Lord's Prayer is powerful in its simplicity.

"*Abba*, Father,
Holy is your Name,
Your Kingdom come.
Our bread for tomorrow / give us today.
And forgive us our debts / as we also herewith forgive our debtors.
And let us not succumb to temptation" (Lk 11:2-4; Mt 6:9-13).[1]

To elaborate upon the theological content of the Our Father would take volumes. But the point we wish to accentuate here is this: the Lord's Prayer is more than a formula, however meaningful that continues to be. The Our Father is also a way of praying, a procedure in praying couched in a series of concretely suggested formulas. The anonymous disciple not only asked for *a* prayer, but also *how* to pray.

Thus Jesus, respecting the propensity of the Semitic mind for concreteness (rather than abstraction), reveals through the formulas of the *Pater Noster* a kind of method in praying

[1]This is a literal translation of J. Jeremias's rendition of what is presumably the oldest wording of the *Pater Noster* in *The Prayers of Jesus* (SCM, 1967), pp. 94-95.

—those qualities which must be present, if "prayer" is to be truly prayer. These characteristics are fundamentally three: (1) adoration ("Abba, Father. . . Holy is Your Name. , , Your Kingdom come"); (2) petition ("Our bread for tomorrow, give us today. . . And let us not succumb to temptation"); (3) contrition ("Forgive us our debts, as we also herewith forgive our debtors").

What is adoration in essence? Adoration brings into explicit consciousness the reality of God to us. We, so to speak, put ourselves in the presence of God. Father, Son and Spirit are always present to us, within us, but we are not always conscious of this truth. So by adoration we explicitly posit this truth before ourselves as personal (reflecting, loving) beings.

What is petition in essence? Petition is the conscious and affective positing of the reality of our total dependence upon the Father — for absolutely everything: from our individual act of existence to the bread we eat and the water we drink. But we are not always explicitly conscious of this dependence. So any petition, be it general or particular, evokes directly our acknowledgement of this all-embracing truth: I am creature utterly dependent upon my loving Father, Creator.

And what is contrition in essence? Contrition is the stark awareness of the actual relationship that exists between God and myself: I am sinner. I am radically alienated from God and from self, set in rebellious opposition to Truth, Goodness and Love. Contrition is facing the basic antagonism between self and God, owning up to my fundamental infidelity which without grace would remain unrepentable. True Christian contrition is the humble and sorrowful surrender of this "nothingness," "dread," "night" to the inscrutable fidelity and loving mercy of Father, Son and Spirit.

Thus Jesus taught his disciples to pray in distinct and successive acts: first, acts of adoration. . .then, acts of petition . . .and finally, acts of contrition. This sequence of acts (first, placing oneself in the presence of God; then, acknowledging one's dependence on him; followed by an ever deeper consciousness of the relationship that exists between self and God) accords particularly well with the usual succession of awareness patterns common to most people. Making specific acts of adoration, petition and contrition is an effective and concrete way of expressing the most basic truth of our existence: God is more lovingly present to me than I am to myself, and before him I am a sinner who is totally dependent on his love and forgiveness.

We may well wonder how Jesus would have responded if the neophyte in Lk 11:1, after practicing for a considerable time the method he had received, could have asked: "Now, Lord, how should I pray?" As this disciple advanced from "beginner" to "proficient" in prayer — to use the terminology of St. John of the Cross[2] — in what direction would his prayer life have evolved? In other words, what constitutes progress in prayer?

Respecting the many different approaches to prayer, John of the Cross synthesized all authentic forms into two general kinds, the first eventually giving way entirely to the second.

---

[2]*Principiantes* ("novices," "apprentices") and *aprovechados* ("those having improved," "those having made progress"). See *Ascent,* II, 13-15; *Night,* I, 8-10. John often uses *el espiritual* (the "spiritual person") for *aprovechado* in the sense of Rm 8:5-17: "spiritual persons are interested in spiritual things."

They are: *discursive prayer* in which the accent is principally on our activity (God working through us), and *contemplative prayer* in which the accent is on our receptivity to the immediate and direct activity of God himself within us.[3]

Progress in prayer, therefore, is characterized by the gradual transformation of distinct and successive acts (adoration... petition...contrition...) into the simplicity of loving surrender. As our prayer life matures, we become increasingly more disinclined towards a multiplicity of discursive acts and ever more inclined towards the wordless, imageless, loving receptivity of contemplation. Our stance before God becomes simply that of "here-I-am."

In its Hebraic sense, "here-I-am" (*hinni*) connotes the attitude of utter receptivity to God.[4] It is the gest of being totally at the disposal of God in silence and mystery, abandoning oneself in dark faith and love to him who forever eludes our grasp.

When Yahweh called him from the burning bush, Moses answered: "Here I am" (Ex 3:4). Isaiah responds to his inaugural vision: "Here I am, send me" (Is 6:9). Mary epitomizes her loving receptivity to God: "Here I am, the servant of

---

[3]John uses phrases like *meditación y discurso, el discursivo meditar, discurrir en la meditación* or simply *el discurso* to designate the "discursiveness" characteristic of the "beginner" in prayer (*idem*). John contrasts this multiplicity of acts (whether exterior or interior) to *contemplación* which characterizes the prayer of the "proficient" or the "spiritual" person (*idem*).

[4]The Hebrew term, in its simplest form *hin-ni*, is composed of the interjection *hen* ("Behold!") with the first person singular suffix *-ni* ("I" or "me"). Thus literally: "Behold me!" or "Lo, I (am here)!"

Yahweh, may it be done to me according to your word" (Lk 1:38).

The Hebrew word *amen* also denotes the unreserved submission of the soul to God, but with the specific nuance of loving, faithful abandonment to the divine initiative.[5] More than a simple "so-be-it," *amen* shouts from the rooftops: "*Fiat.* Here I am: naked, poor, wholly yours."

Far more than just "words," both *hinni* and *amen* are in a very real sense all-expressive gestures, all-embracing attitudes.

Several prayerful utterances of Jesus are preserved for us in the Gospel. While each logion in its own way reflects his inner attitude of *hinni*, of *amen*, two prayers do so with particular force: "*Abba*, Father, if it is your will, take this cup away from me. Nevertheless, let your will be done, not mine" (Lk 22:42; Mk 14:36; Mt 26:39-42). And "*Abba*, Father, into your hands I commit my spirit" (Lk 23:46). Even though "a prayer" is sometimes verbalized by Jesus which is overheard by another — oftentimes meant to be overheard by someone else — most of the prayer of Jesus transpired in solitude: "He would always go off to some place where he could be alone and pray" (Lk 5:16).

What do you suppose Jesus *did* during his solitary prayer? What do you suppose he *said* or *thought* while praying?

He did *nada* during his solitary prayer. Jesus said nothing, thought nothing while praying. What could he do that he was

[5]*Amen* is the interjection derived from the verb *aman*, meaning "to stay, to support," and intransitively "to be firm, true, faithful." Thus, as a noun *amen* can mean "truth, faithfulness, steadfastness," and as an adverb "verily, truly, indeed." See Dt 7:9; 27:15; Ps 41:13; 106:48; Jn 5:19,25; Rv 3:14; 5:14.

not already doing? What word (audible or mental) could he say or think that would not be superfluous — he is the Word of the Father, incarnate.

Well then, if he did nothing, said nothing, thought nothing in solitary prayer, what took place? Jesus surely was not in some sort of suspended animation or self-hypnotic trance. What was transpiring?

St. Paul gives us the key: *kenosis*, "He emptied himself" (Ph 2:7). In the context of the prayer of Jesus, "kenosis" means that he opened and surrendered himself in order that his divinity could more and more permeate his humanity. Jesus is truly God and truly man, hypostatically united from the moment of his conception. Nevertheless, his humanity —just like ours — was not complete until the moment of his personal death on the cross. Consequently, it is only in the resurrection that his humanity — like ours — could become completely deified, divinized.

During prayer then Jesus was allowing himself par excellence to be opened more and more intensely to his own divine transforming activity. He was anticipating — not just preparing for — the definitive surrender of his whole being to the Father in death.

So it was for Christ. So it must also be for us. Yet with this important distinction: whereas Jesus emptied *himself* (active-reflexive) because of the hypostatic union, we *are emptied* (passively) by God. As a matter of historical fact, God has actually communicated himself through only one way: Jesus Christ, by way of kenosis (Ph 2:7). Consequently, there is only one "way" that we can commune with him — the same "way": by *being emptied*. Thus Christ welling up in the soul, divinizing it, empties it of all that cannot be transformed into himself.

What then is the soul's basic attitude and response vis-à-vis this process of sanctification? What else can it be, but one of loving receptivity to undergo God, one of loving openness to endure God, one of loving passivity to suffer God — an attitude of simply being in love with Father, Son and Spirit.

Progress in prayer is in no way the product of our initiative or our effort: "You did not choose me. No, I chose you." (Jn 15:16) Progress in prayer depends rather on our faithful response to God's initiative. Any misguided attempts to induce contemplation or to accelerate the process of spiritualization by shortcuts, methods or techniques only impede progress. Through our daily fidelity to the spontaneous movements of God within us, he leads us to lovingly surrender our self to himself in his way, in his time, and in a manner we often cannot even recognize, much less fathom: "For my thoughts are not your thoughts; my ways not your ways — it is Yahweh who speaks!" (Is 55:8).

For some this contemplative threshold may come early in life after little effort at discursive prayer. For others it may come only after a lifetime of struggling through various discursive methods. Generally however, the readiness of heart to encounter God immediately and directly in contemplation presupposes a consistency and perseverance in sustained effort at some discursive prayer for a considerable length of time.

4

True Contemplation

Illusions associated with the term "contemplation" obscure the true place of contemplative prayer in the process of transformation. Frequently, mistaken notions originate in the superficial reading of the mystics, and/or in the study of only random excerpts from spiritual authors. Often what is basically sound doctrine is misinterpreted because of failure to distinguish universally applicable principles from that which is peculiar to the mystic's own experience and culture. At times illusions are perpetuated by writers who have only a certain intellectual knowledge of mystical realities, but lack sufficient personal experience in these matters. And there are those works which so accentuate personal experience that basic principles of ascetical-mystical theology are sadly neglected.

Contemplation is sometimes falsely equated with a kind of "spiritual high" wherein the soul acquires precise knowledge of who God is, accompanied by a clear perception of his immediate presence. God in himself cannot be grasped by anything sensible or intellectual. Contemplation is that leap in faith by which we encounter God *beyond* anything perceptible, and it is by its very nature purgative: "As fire consumes the tarnish and rust of metal, so contemplation annihilates, empties and consumes all the affections and imperfect habits that the soul has contracted throughout its life. Since these imperfections are deeply rooted in the substance of the soul, it usually suffers, in addition to its poverty and spiritual emptiness, an oppressive undoing and inner torment."[1]

Neither is contemplation the blocking out of all perceptible reality in order to remain empty. The mere absence of thoughts, emotions, activity or distractions does not constitute prayer of any kind. The inducement of such a self-made void leads the soul not into the solitude of God but into withdrawal from reality: "One who does this of set purpose . . . simply enters into an artificial darkness of his own making. He is not alone with God, but alone with himself. He is not in the presence of the Transcendent One, but of an idol: his own complacent identity. He becomes immersed and lost in himself, in a state of inert, primitive and infantile narcissism."[2]

The replacement of discursive meditation with the self-imposed activity of maintaining a blank, undistracted mind has no intrinsic value whatsoever relative to God. Moreover, it could have harmful effects on all aspects of personality development.

[1]*Night*, II, 6, 5.

[2]CP, p. 90.

At times contemplation is confused with the experience of such spiritual phenomena as visions, locutions and levitations. This inaccurate association is often further compounded by preconceived, naive ideas of how these special graces should occur. While some type of spiritual phenomenon may be granted on rare occasion, such a grace must always be distinguished from contemplation itself. God may choose to grant a person a spiritual gift without that person having yet crossed the threshold of contemplation. And God may bestow the infinitely more important grace of contemplation without ever granting spiritual phenomena at all.

Actually, it is the universal teaching of the mystics that spiritual phenoména should neither be desired nor sought after since attachment to them hinders interior progress. Even should God grant such graces, the soul's attitude towards them must remain one of humility and detachment. In fact, rather than engaging in prolonged discernment as to their authenticity, the soul should let go such experiences and continue its journey in dark faith. "God does not demand that these souls undertake this labor" of discernment, "nor does he desire that ordinary, simple persons be put in this conflict and danger, for they have safe and sound teaching, which is faith, wherein they can go forward."[3]

The above are some of the more common illusions associated with contemplative prayer — what contemplation is not! But what *is* contemplation?

In order to appreciate properly the response to this question, the reader must diligently keep in mind the fact that we are in the realm of sheer faith, of utter mystery where spiritual

[3]*Ascent*, II, 16, 14. See *Ascent*, II, 10-32.

things can only be taught spiritually (1 Co 2:13). Consequently, contemplation by the very nature of its depth and simplicity must always transcend any attempt at description: "Who can describe the understanding God gives to loving souls in whom he dwells? And who can express the experience he imparts to them? Who could ever explain the desire he gives them? Certainly no one can. Not even the very souls through whom he passes."[4]

Contemplation is the immediately transforming and directly consuming activity of God himself within the soul calling forth its voluntary undergoing of that transformation and purgation in love and faith.[5] It is a silent, imageless and loving communion with God himself which transcends all discursiveness. "Contemplation is none other than a secret, peaceful and loving infusion of God which, if the soul allows it to happen, enflames it in the spirit of love."[6] Most simply, contemplation is being loved by God himself from within oneself and loving him with all one's being in return: *Estarse*

---

[4]*Canticle, Prologue,* 1. "I do not believe that anyone who has not had such experience will understand this well. Yet the soul experiencing this is aware that what it has so sublimely experienced remains beyond its understanding. It therefore calls this an 'I-don't-know-what' (*un no-sé-qué*). Since it is not understandable, it is indescribable, although the soul knows that it has experienced it (*se sabe sentir*)" (*Canticle,* 7, 10).

[5]See *Night,* II, 5, 1.

[6]*Night,* I, 10, 6. The contemplative soul "must be content simply with a loving and peaceful attentiveness in God (*advertencia amorosa y sosegada en Dios*), being without concern, without effort, and even without desire to taste him or feel him" in any way (*idem,* I, 10, 4).

amando al Amado — "Remaining loving one's Beloved."[7]

P. Teilhard de Chardin expresses well the attitude of the contemplative soul: "To lose oneself in the Unfathomable, to plunge into the Inexhaustible, to find peace in the Incorruptible. . .to give of one's deepest to him whose depth has no end."[8]

In contemplation we abide in mystery, always receptive to being led in love by God along a way we cannot know.

Two biblical images — "listen" and "come" — frequently express what we call "contemplation." At times these images are used singly:

> "Listen to my voice, then I will be your God and you will be my people" (Jr 7:23).
> "Come to me. . .and I will refresh you" (Mt 11:28).

At other times both images are interwoven in the same passage:

> "Come. . . . Listen, listen to me. . . . Come to me. Listen and your soul will live" (Is 55:1-3).
> "The Spirit and the Bride say, 'Come.' Let everyone who listens answer, 'Come'" (Rv 22:17).

What does it mean "to listen"? "Speak, Lord, your servant is listening" (1 S 3:1-11); "Give your servant a listening heart" (1 K 3:9); "This is my beloved Son. . . . Listen to him" (Lk 9:35).

---

[7]John of the Cross, *Sum of Perfection*, 4. *Estarse* is usually translated by "to stay, remain," but literally it means "to be oneself."

[8]DM, pp. 127-128.

Listening is distinguished from hearing. One hears noises, sounds, things. But one listens to a person. Listening is being lovingly attentive to the other's person, irrespective of words or actions. To listen is to commune lovingly with the other whether anything is said or heard at all.

Listening to God does not mean expecting a specific communication, a certain kind of knowledge, a particular message. One simply listens — listens to God, without listening *for* any-*thing.*

Listening in the biblical sense, like loving, has within itself its own reason for being. That is, you do not need a reason or a purpose to listen. You do not have to listen "in order that . . ." You just listen! You commune lovingly with your Beloved in naked abandonment — so abandoned in fact that the soul must let go all desire to see, to feel, to hear, to understand, to experience any-*thing* whatsoever in prayer.[9] Listening is simply waiting upon God in himself in loving expectancy, in loving openness, without desiring any-*thing.*

Of course, on occasion, something may happen while listening. At times in deep prayer one may hear something, so to speak. One may sometimes understand better or feel something. Whether one does or does not have any sensory accompaniment in prayer is entirely the "Father's business' (Lk 2:49). That depends uniquely upon the will of God in each given situation. Nor is it better one way or the other (that is, experiencing something or experiencing *nada*). What is of utmost importance, however, is that the soul remain listening, detached from all desire to hear or feel anything in prayer.

[9]See *CP*, pp. 89-95; *Night*, 1, 9, 6-9 and 1, 10, 4-6.

This is indeed a most difficult truth to assimilate, namely: "The contemplative is one who would rather not know than know. . . . Rather not have proof that God loves him."[10]

In particular biblical contexts, the verb "come" often connotes two qualities essential to contemplation: nakedness and receptivity. "Come to the water all you who are thirsty. Though you have no money, come!" (Is 55:1). That is: Come exactly as you are — poor, stripped, naked, without anything — just come! Simply be who you are: a struggling sinner, desperately in need of God's loving mercy. You don't need any-*thing* to help you be. You don't need any tricks, any gimmicks, any make-up — only poverty of spirit. You don't need to be perfect either. You don't even need to be good. Simply be the poor one that you are, and come. Let yourself be drawn by me, into me. For, "I shall draw all to myself" (Jn 12:32).

As God intensifies the contemplative element in each soul — its poverty, its receptivity, its capacity to love — he invites it to come, to listen, to be ever more free: "The Spirit and the Bride say, 'Come.' Let everyone who listens answer, 'Come.' Then let all who are thirsty come: all who want it may have the water of life and have it free" (Rv 22:17).

God dwelling within the soul incites in it an insatiable thirsting for himself as he is in himself, and freely invites the soul to interpersonal communion with himself. He calls us to come, to remain in rest and quietude, free from the burden and labor of all activity, lovingly attentive to him. When this invitation is perceived in faith, those listening respond by

[10]CP, p. 89.

letting God come forth within themselves. We let him well up in our being by remaining receptive to his transforming and consuming love.

5

The Function of the Faculties

Jesus instructed his disciples: "When you pray, go to your private room and, when you have shut your door, pray to your Father who is in that secret place, and your Father who sees all that is done in secret will reward you" (Mt 6:6).

In contemplation we enter into the private room of the heart. God closes the door of our faculties to particular images and concepts so that we can experience in secret him who dwells hiddenly within. Nevertheless, our faculties do have an important function in an integrated life of prayer.

The faculties of the soul are the media through which we normally communicate with creation, and in the beginning of our prayer life they are the usual means through which we commune with God also. Our most spiritual faculties —

intellect, memory and will[1] — have under their influence other faculties: imagination, emotions, sight, hearing, touch, etc. These deal with the more sensory aspects of the human person.[2]

In the usual process of knowing and loving, the exterior senses form impressions through their contact with reality. These impressions are then picked up by the imagination and shaped into images, which in turn are passed on to the intellect where the essence of the image is spiritualized into an idea or concept. From a particular idea, the intellect can then proceed to formulate other concepts. On the basis of the knowledge the intellect acquires, the will exercises its power to love and to make choices.

In discursive meditation, the faculties operate along the lines of the process of knowing and willing described above. Through the use of such discursive material as scriptural passages, nature, specific acts of adoration, petition, thanksgiv-

---

[1] Following Augustine, John of the Cross enumerates the basic spiritual faculties of the soul as: intellect (*Ascent*, II, 8-32), memory (*Ascent*, III, 1-15) and will (*Ascent*, III, 16-45).

[2] In the mind of John of the Cross all the faculties, spiritual and sensory alike, pertain to what he calls "the sensory part of the soul" (see *Ascent*, I, 1, 2; *Night*, II, 3). John does not speak of the sensory part of the *body*. Thus, he distinguishes *in the soul* a sensory or observable aspect — we might say "the outer person" — from the spiritual or deepest aspect: the "inner person." In the terminology of John, therefore, the intellect, memory and will (even though they are "spiritual" faculties) pertain to the sensory part of the soul and to the "night of sense." The "night of spirit," the purgation of the "spiritual part of the soul," pertains principally to the purification of that mysterious "self" which is beyond all the faculties as such.

ing, God gives a particular knowledge *of* himself and moves the will to love him more. By providing various sensory consolations, God draws the memory,[3] the intellect and the will away from their usual attractions and gradually directs them more and more towards spirit.

In contemplation, however, the function of these faculties is transformed. In contemplative prayer God communes directly and immediately with the soul, from within the soul. In discursive prayer God communes indirectly and through media with the soul, from within or from without. Discursiveness is usually characterized by one or any combination of these three possibilities: I speak with myself about God. I speak with God about myself. I speak with God about himself. In all instances there is an "about," a medium of exchange between God and the soul. Contemplation in a sense is the removal by God of "about." All that remains is God and the soul directly communing one with the other.

Thus, God makes the soul capable of receiving himself immediately (i.e., without medium). This direct communion empties and deprives the faculties of all particular concepts, objects and considerations. Our faculties are no longer occupied with specific thoughts, emotions or acts (be they exterior or interior) as means of communication with God. Rather our faculties are drawn by him into a simple act of love: "At this

---

[3]Following Augustine, John of the Cross uses "memory" (*memoria*) to mean much more than simply recalling the past. Augustine uses this term to denote the insatiable yearning of the soul for God, the love-drive toward the Absolute. It is basically *memoria* which he describes in *Confessions*, I, 1: "You have made us for yourself alone, O Lord, and our heart is restless until it rests in you." See *idem*, X, 8-25.

stage, the faculties are at rest. They work not actively, but passively by receiving what God is effecting in them."[4]

Because the initiative comes entirely from God, any attempt at this time to make memory, intellect or will function as in discursive prayer will only hinder God's way of accomplishing his will in us. "The reason for this is that in this state of contemplation, when the soul leaves discursive meditation and enters the state of proficients, *it is now God who is working in the soul*. He therefore binds the interior faculties and leaves no support in the intellect, no satisfaction in the will, no discourse in the memory. At this time a soul's efforts are of no avail, but rather are an obstacle to the interior peace and work which God is accomplishing in the spirit through that dryness of sense."[5]

What a person is usually conscious of in contemplation is a general, vague state of emptiness in which no-thing in particular is present. Yet, in this emptiness there is often the intuitive awareness, very subtle and delicate, that somehow something is transpiring even though we do not know specifically what or how: "We generally know that something is going on, but we cannot tell anyone else, or even tell ourselves, what it is, because we only describe by images. Hence, when we reflect upon it, and try to put it into words, we can only call it 'nothing' or vacancy; only we *know* that 'nothing' really means 'the ALL'."[6]

[4]*Ascent*, II, 12, 8.

[5]*Night*, I, 9, 7. Emphasis is our own.

[6]John Chapman, *Spiritual Letters* (Sheed, 1938), p. 94.

However, while the intellect does not receive a particular knowledge in contemplation, it does receive a general, loving, intuitive knowledge of God.[7] Perhaps an analogy would shed some light on this. When two persons are in love, they know each other directly in and through love. Loving knowledge is experiential, and as such is much more profound than simply knowing about the other. Loving knowledge means experiencing in love that which most uniquely constitutes the other as person. This kind of knowledge is sometimes called intuitive since it is derived from love, in love, rather than from the processes of cognition. As such, it leads the person by "unknowing" to an experience of the beloved which is beyond all ability to grasp the other. That is, the mystery of the other is experienced really as mystery. As love matures, this loving knowledge becomes more and more ineffable, yet unmistakable.

Something similar occurs in our loving encounter with God. We become ever more intuitively conscious of the mystery of God and at the same time pass through an unknowing of what we had previously conceptualized him to be. We experience that no matter how loving, wise, gentle, or just we may have perceived him to be, no image conveys him as he is in himself. While there is a certain truth in our conceptualizations of him, he is still never who we say he is

---

[7]It is very difficult to find terms not open to misunderstanding which express what we are attempting to describe. In this context, John of the Cross frequently uses expressions like the following: *noticia general, amorosa, confusa, pacifica,* (Ascent, II, 13-15); *inteligencia oscura y general* (Ascent, II, 10, 4); *advertencia amorosa, sosegada, sencilla* (*Night*, I, 10, 4 and *Flame*, 3, 34); *ciencia secreta* (*Canticle*, 27, 5).

because he is always infinitely more. We experience him in love as *un-no-sé-qué*.[8]

Thus the general, loving knowledge which the intellect receives in contemplation consists paradoxically in knowing more who God is not than who he is. This is knowing by way of kenosis (Ph 2:7); in other words, knowing by unknowing.

Our knowing by unknowing transpires in the darkness of faith without going through any process of reasoning, analyzing or synthesizing. In fact, because this general, loving knowledge does not consist in anything precise or definite, we may not even be aware of receiving it: "This general knowledge (*noticia general*) is at times so subtle and delicate — particularly when it is most pure, simple and perfect, most spiritual and most interior — that the soul does not perceive it or feel it, even though it is engaged in it."[9]

John of the Cross goes on to explain that this is most frequently the case when this loving knowledge is in itself most clear and simple, as well as when the soul itself is most purified of particular kinds of knowledge and intelligence which the understanding or the senses might seize upon. In other words, the more spiritual and of greater intrinsic value is this general, loving knowledge, the less perceptible it becomes to the intellect. Yet when it is less spiritual and somewhat perceptible, the intellect often judges it to be more spiritual and of greater value than it really is: "For when this knowledge is purest and simplest and most perfect, the understanding (*entendimiento*) is least conscious of it and thinks of it as most

[8]"An I-don't-know-what" (*Canticle*, 7, 9-10).

[9]*Ascent*, II, 14, 8.

obscure. On the other hand, the less pure and simple this"
general, loving "knowledge is the clearer and more important
it appears to the understanding, since it is clothed in, mingled
with or immersed in certain intelligible forms upon which the
understanding or sense may seize."[10]

Needless to say, the soul can so very easily misinterpret
God's signs at this threshold of the grace of contemplation.
The truth of the matter is so contrary to what the soul thinks
or assumes it should be.

Love is unquestionably the core of contemplation. Love
—God loving the soul and the soul loving him in response —
is the most fundamental characteristic of contemplation as
well as the source of all that flows from it. What is deepest in
the human person is permeated by love. Thus, it is within our
innermost self that Father, Son and Spirit dwell in love.[11]

Even though strictly speaking it is the whole human person
who receives this contemplative grace, still it is correct to
single out the will as the faculty par excellence where this
grace transpires with particular intensity.

In contemplation the will is acted upon by God in such a
way as to love God with his very own love. In contemplation
our only desire is to be loved by him and to love him with all
our being in return. However, since this loving exchange
transpires in an ever increasingly spiritual manner, it is gener-

---

[10]*Ascent*, II, 14, 8.

[11]In one of his most theologically reflective statements on the "divine
indwelling," John phrases it this way: "The Word . . . together with the
Father and the Holy Spirit is hidden in essence and in presence (*essencial y
presencialmente*) in the intimate being (*en el íntimo ser*) of the soul" (*Canticle*,
1, 6).

ally experienced without any particular feeling or emotion. The will — the whole person — remains loving the Beloved in darkness and emptiness, without distinct knowledge of him: "Just as general, loving knowledge is communicated obscurely to the intellect, so too knowledge and love are given confusedly to the will without it knowing distinctly what it loves."[12]

In résumé, the basic difference between the function of the intellect and the function of the will in discursive meditation and contemplation is this: In discursive meditation the intellect employs images and concepts derived from sensory perceptions in order to move the will to love God. In contemplation the intellect and will, having been drawn directly by God into his transforming activity, receive immediately the love which God effects in them.

To the soul who finds the discursive activity of its faculties beginning to cease because it is being led into contemplation, John of the Cross gives this word of advice: "The soul should not mind if the operations of its faculties are being lost to it. It ought rather to desire that this happen quickly so that the soul, not obstructing the operation of infused contemplation which God is bestowing, may receive it with more peaceful abundance and make room in its spirit for the enkindling and burning of the love that this dark and secret contemplation brings with it and sets firmly in the soul."[13]

Actually it is only in contemplation that the memory, the intellect and the will begin to reach their full potential: "The

[12]*Ascent*, II, 14, 12. See *Night*, II, 9, 3.

[13]*Night*, I, 10, 6.

capacity of these caverns is deep; for that which they are capable of containing, which is God, is deep and infinite. Therefore, in a certain sense their capacity is infinite, their thirst is infinite, their hunger also is deep and infinite, and their languishing and pain are infinite death."[14]

[14]*Flame*, 3, 22.

6

Principles of Discernment

It is very important to interior growth that a person know when to let go discursive meditation in order to enter into contemplation. It is God himself who brings the soul through this threshold at the right time and in the proper measure. Yet the faithful response of the soul to this initiative is also essential. On the one hand, to cling to discursive prayer after God has indicated that the soul should pass beyond it can hinder his transforming activity. On the other hand, to try to abandon discursiveness before God has finished using its benefits in the soul can impede the workings of grace.

What then are the basic "signs that a spiritual person must find within himself whereby he can discern the appropriate time to leave meditation and discursiveness in order to pass on to the state of contemplation"?[1]

While St. John of the Cross is by no means the first spiritual author to treat of these signs, he is nonetheless the first to synthesize them so succinctly. He presents three fundamental indications which must be simultaneously present in the soul for the discernment of an authentic call to contemplative prayer: (1) the inability to meditate discursively on God as was one's previous habit, (2) a disinclination to fix one's imagination and senses upon other particular objects, (3) the desire to enter more frequently and for longer periods into solitary, affective prayer.[2]

(1) "The first sign is the realization that the soul can no longer meditate or discourse with the imagination, nor can it find meaningfulness" in these procedures "as before. On the contrary, it now finds aridity where previously it could fix its senses and derive great satisfaction. However, to the degree that the soul still finds some satisfaction and can still discourse in meditation, it should not abandon this form of prayer."

[1] *Ascent*, II, 13, 1-9. The same reference holds for all quoted passages in this chapter, unless otherwise identified. Note that for John these are not only signs of discernment, but are also *conditions* of interior growth. That is, unless they occur, the progress of the "proficient" is not possible.

[2] In his *Dichos de luz y amor* John presents an even more concise expression of "the signs of interior recollection: The first is when the soul lacks satisfaction (*no gusta*) in passing things. The second is when it desires (*gusta*) solitude, silence and attentiveness to all that is more perfect. The third is when the things that used to help it now hinder it — things like considerations, meditations and acts — so that now the soul brings to prayer no other support than faith, hope and charity" (n. 118). See *Flame*, 3, 39.

In other words, the soul perceives within itself an inability to pray, as well as a general lack of meaningfulness in relation to its previous habits and experiences in prayer — and this for no particular reason of which the soul is aware. Usually this realization is both gradual (over a period of time) and comparative (I may still be able to meditate some, but not as easily nor as well as I used to. I may still find some meaningfulness in novenas and litanies, but not nearly as much as before.)

There are some souls, however, who have never been able to engage satisfactorily in much discursiveness. In their case the elements of time-lapse and comparison are hardly applicable. Moreover, this "inability" and the "loss of satisfaction" need not be absolute, so to speak. It suffices for this sign that they be relative, that they come and go, that they be more or less intense.

Over the long run, however, both the inability as well as the loss of meaningfulness will increase eventually to the point of complete abandonment of the particular method of prayer in view of contemplation. Even in those instances where the particular form of prayer may not be abandoned as such (e.g., the Eucharist, examination of conscience), in the advanced stages of contemplation these prayer forms are nevertheless transformed.

When the inability to meditate is truly from God, the soul simply cannot carry on as before, no matter how much effort it puts into it. Oftentimes the more effort exerted in trying to return to previous satisfaction or ability in discursiveness, the more frustrating and unfulfilling the venture becomes.

A soul usually perceives the presence of this first sign within itself when it experiences during prayer (frequently with some perplexity and guilt feelings) not only difficulty in fixing its attention discursively on God (and on the things of God),[3] but also an actual disinclination to do so. For example, a soul habituated to the Ignation method of meditation upon scriptural passages will discover a mysterious inclination to put aside the Bible, at least for awhile, and simply remain still in God. Something similar may occur to someone given to the recitation of the Divine Office, to shared prayer, to Charismatic meetings, even to the simple repetition of ejaculations. The soul spontaneously wants to remain quiet.

St. John of the Cross's advice in these instances is this: let it happen. That is, just remain still ("unable" and "disinclined") for as long as you want. Then go back to your discursiveness, but only to the extent that you really can and desire to do so — not just because you believe that you *should* do so. Always pray as you can, not as you think you should.

However, since this inability and disinclination to meditate on God (and on the things of God) can also arise from illness, fatigue, laziness or personal sin, a second sign and condition must be discerned together with the first.

(2) "The second sign is that the soul experiences no desire to fix its imagination or senses on other particular things, exterior or interior."

---

[3]John of the Cross uses this expression, "the things of God" (*las cosas de Dios*), to designate any-*thing* and every-*thing* that is from God, to God, of God, about God, "on" God, but is not actually God himself in himself. This includes such "supernatural" and "spiritual" creatures as the sacraments and the charisms. (See *Canticle*, 1-7; *Ascent*, II, 1, 1 and III, 2, 3; *Night*, I, 11, 1 and II, 16, 1).

Besides being unable to meditate as before and disinclined to fix its attention on concepts, ideas or things of God, the soul is also disinclined to center its attentiveness purposely on any other particular thing whatsoever, whether it be an exterior object of interest or interior fantasies. The truly contemplative soul is not drawn intentionally during prayer to any form of daydreaming, be it deliberately reliving cherished moments, idly admiring nature or planning for the future. The inclination to abandon discursive prayer for the purpose of fixing one's attention on something other than the things of God indicates that the inability to meditate may be originating from causes other than contemplation.

Even though a soul does not pursue these extraneous thoughts of set purpose, it often finds itself being bombarded by one tangent after another. Actually this phenomenon is quite normal, even in rather advanced contemplative prayer. When God is making the soul more receptive to his transforming love, he empties the intellect of all particular concepts. As this occurs, much in the soul's unconscious which it was previously too occupied to face comes gushing forth into consciousness. Thus a person given more to contemplation than to discursiveness is paradoxically more prone to barrages of distractions, tangents and temptations during actual prayer.[4]

John of the Cross puts it this way: "I do not say that the imagination does not come and go in contemplation — it usually wanders quite freely even in deep recollection — but

[4]See Thomas Merton, *New Seeds of Contemplation* (New Directions, 1961), pp. 221-224; *Cloud*, 7, 8, 26, 32, 33; Jean Pierre de Caussade, *Abandonment to Divine Providence*, 2, 4, letters 8 & 15; 2, 6, letter 20.

rather that the soul does not enjoy fixing itself purposely on extraneous things." That is, rather than giving the soul pleasure and delight, these distractions and tangents cause it concern.

Of itself nothing transpiring on a perceptible level during contemplation can disturb God's loving activity in the depths of our being. But *we* can disturb him if we do not handle these distractions properly. This is similar to the situation in the Gospel when Jesus was asleep in the boat while a violent tempest broke over the lake (Mk 4:35-41; Lk 8:22-25). The "storm" did not bother Jesus in the least. He was so calm that he remained sleeping, but the disciples were so frightened that they awakened him. Thus the disciples themselves — not the storm — disturbed Jesus. His response to them (and to us) is: "Why are you so distraught? Oh, you of little faith!" (Mt 8:26).

How then might we effectively deal with these barrages? Obviously we should not foster or deliberately entertain them. But neither should we try to fight them directly, since this would require putting our attention on them (and on self) rather than remaining lovingly attentive towards God in himself.

In discursive prayer we counteract a distraction by getting our mind back on the subject (that is, we replace one thought with another). However, in contemplation where we are not deliberately trying to think or not to think, we counter these barrages most effectively by suffering them, by letting them run their course, all the while keeping our affective attentiveness riveted on God.

At times it may be helpful to repeat slowly an ejaculatory

prayer: for instance, "Abba, Father, I love you" or simply "Jesus." These affective "words" sometimes help to offset the wordiness of the tangents as they persist. Yet, oftentimes nothing we can do really allays these storms as they come one after the other. In this case we must just endure them, persevering in prayer. In faith we must abandon ourselves lovingly to the transforming activity of God within us.

Nevertheless, since the disinclination to fix one's attention on any extraneous object may arise from certain personality disorders, a third sign and condition must be present together with the first and the second.

(3) "The third and surest sign is that the soul enjoys (*gusta*) remaining alone with loving attentiveness towards God, without" being focused on any "particular consideration, in interior peace, quietude and rest, without acts and exercises of the faculties of memory, intellect and will — at least discursive acts wherein one proceeds from one point to another."

The third sign is the desire to be alone, waiting upon God with a loving expectancy, a peaceful attentiveness, a listening heart. The inclination towards solitude, while being primarily an interior reality, manifests itself in an increasing desire for exterior solitude as well. The soul finds itself irresistibly drawn to the stillness of a small chapel, to a solitary spot in nature or to some other secluded place "in order to be alone and pray" (Lk 5:16).

This third sign is the "surest" (*la más cierta*) since it is this arid contemplation already in progress that causes the inability to meditate as well as the disinclination to think of God or of anything created.

7

Further Principles of Discernment

Once he brings the soul through the threshold of contemplative prayer, God, in and through contemplation, causes a radical intensification of the "dark night."[1] The experience of night is in no way confined to specific periods of prayer. It is rather an all-pervasive reality which permeates every detail of our personal lives. The phase of night corresponding to the beginning of contemplation is the "night of sense."

In the night of sense God leads the soul beyond the realm of empirical certitude and clarity in order to experience him

[1] There are many facets to the *noche oscura* of John of the Cross. Basically however, what he understands by "night" is "the privation of gratification in the appetite regarding all things" (*la privación del gusto en el apetito de todas las cosas*: Ascent, I, 3, 1 and 4). Or again: "This dark night is an influence of God within the soul which purges it of its ignorances and

more truly in spirit and in more profound faith. He thus deprives the soul of its previous consolation and satisfaction leaving it in aridity, emptiness, confusion and even in doubt as to whether it is being faithful to him at all. "God leaves them in such darkness that they do not know which way to turn with their imagination and discursiveness for they cannot advance in meditation as they did previously. . . . God leaves them in such dryness that they not only fail to experience satisfaction and enjoyment in the spiritual things and good works in which they had formerly found their delights and pleasures, but now on the contrary they find that they can no longer be satisfied or derive enjoyment at all. . . . This change is very disconcerting for them, because everything seems to be functioning in reverse."[2]

This night of sense, which accompanies and results from the beginning of contemplation, is a very trying and often prolonged experience for the soul. This night is very difficult to discern not only because of the confusion and doubts which it quite normally engenders, but also because many of its indications are similar, at least on the surface, to symptoms related to personality disorders, psychotic disturbances and/or moral lassitude. Therefore, very enlightened and careful discernment is necessary in order to distinguish depression, dissipation, boredom, moodiness, laziness and mediocrity from the authentic, God-influenced night of sense.

imperfections, whether they be habitual, natural or spiritual. This is called infused contemplation. . . . In this" night-contemplation "God secretly teaches the soul and instructs it in the perfection of love, without the soul doing anything or understanding how it is taking place" (*Night*, II, 5, 1).

[2]*Night*, I, 8, 3.

St. John of the Cross synthesizes three universal principles of discernment which, when present together, indicate that the soul is authentically undergoing the night of sense As well as being signs which furnish positive indication of this divine influence within the soul, these principles are also necessary conditions for the transformation of each soul "into the likeness of Christ" (2 Co 3:18).

The three universal signs and conditions "whereby a spiritual person can discern whether he/she is travelling this road of night and purgation of sense" are these: (1) aridity across the board, (2) a certain interior anxiety and (3) the irresistible drawing into a more contemplative stance during prayer.[3]

The three signs of the *Night* differ from the three signs of the *Ascent*. The principal difference lies in the fact that John is addressing himself to slightly different questions in each instance. In the *Ascent* he is concerned with the transition to contemplative prayer as such, whereas in the *Night* he treats more generally of the contemplative thrust of one's life at a threshold particularly difficult to discern. John distributes the gist of signs #1, #2, #3 of the *Ascent* in signs #1 and #3 of the *Night*, and then explicates a further sign which becomes #2 in the latter.

(1) "The first sign is that just as the soul does not find satisfaction or consolation in the things of God, it does not find it in anything else created either."

The first sign and condition is the experience of aridity across the board. The soul finds within itself not only a lack of

---

[3]*Night*, 1, 1-9. The same reference holds true for all other quoted passages in this chapter, unless otherwise identified.

satisfaction and consolation in spiritual realities, but also a lack of satisfaction and consolation in all the concrete particulars of life. The same kind of meaningfulness that was previously experienced (for example, in particular methods of prayer, in the celebration of the Eucharist, in family or community life, in various religious customs and devotions, in personal relationships or ministry) is no longer present.

The soul quickly discovers that this void within itself cannot be filled, as possibly it was before, by simply changing to a new form of recreation, another community, a more exciting ministry, a different method of prayer. Not even a second honeymoon or a newly remodeled home seems to assuage the intensity of this dryness or rekindle the ardor of previous enthusiasm. Nothing seems to work anymore. That strange, gnawing void within persists however much the soul tries to elude it.

Why? From where does it arise? "God sets the soul in this dark night in order to dry up and purge its sensory appetite. He does not let it find attraction or delight in anything whatsoever."

While it may appear to some undergoing this aridity that their lives are now dominated by a strange sense of general dissatisfaction, such is not in fact the case. If the sense of all-pervasive emptiness which they experience is indeed from God — true aridity, in other words — then this is not "dissatisfaction" but rather the inability ever again to be satisfied. Dissatisfaction — being bored and discontent with life — arises from a negative attitude, a tendency towards isolation. The aridity of the dark night, on the contrary, arises from the positive experience of our inability to be fully satisfied by anything or anyone other than God in himself. Aridity springs forth from an intense zest for life — for life in the fullest, at its Source.

The soul's experience of Its inability to be satisfied normally comes through its involvement in and with creation. It does not come through disappointment with this involvement or with the quality thereof, but rather as a necessary development of this effort. In this way creation fulfills to its maximum its positive, providential role in our divinization. In this manner creation forces us to learn that it cannot satisfy our deepest longing and desires, and in so doing it points us beyond itself, opening our hearts to the Infinite by way of kenosis.

However, it does happen frequently that some dissatisfaction as well as some inability to be satisfied — that is, both some selfishness and some spiritual maturity — are operative in the same situation at the same time. In these instances it behooves the soul to discern which is the predominant influence: boredom or aridity, loneliness or aloneness, self or the Other, withdrawal or with-All, isolation or solitude.

Integral to the experience of aridity across the board is a radical change in our value system. (One of the characteristics of maturation is that the exteriorly imposed value system of a child becomes interiorized and personalized through adolescence and adulthood.) In the night of sense, we are challenged to take the risk of assuming personal responsibility for all our actions and decisions. There is a decisive movement away from a quantitative value system towards the way of pure quality. No longer can we assess our progress primarily by how well we measure up to the letter of the law, to rules, regulations and customs. With the gradual shift away from clarity and precision to mystery and ineffability, the ultimate criterion for all true spiritual progress becomes increasingly the quality of our *love*.

The presence of aridity across the board indicates that very likely the soul is being led by God into the night of sense. However, since an apparently similar kind of emptiness can have its origin in quite other sources such as dissipation, lassitude, personal sin, personality disorders and/or psychosis, a second sign and condition is necessary.

(2) "The second sign for the discernment of this purgation is that the memory ordinarily turns to God with solicitude and with painful care, thinking that it is not serving God but backsliding, because it experiences this inability to derive satisfaction from the things of God."

Unaccustomed to this aridity in all things, the soul is thrown into a state of anxious, painful questioning. The elusive world of mystery into which the night thrusts it is so unfamiliar that the soul does not know whether it is entering more deeply into its commitment to Christ or whether it has begun to backslide. Experiencing an obvious loss of meaningfulness regarding such key factors as its value system, its enthusiasm and its spiritual gusto, the soul now fears that it is heading towards spiritual bankruptcy. Even though it desires so much to serve God and makes such a sincere effort to do so, the soul agonizes whether or not it is truly remaining faithful. Failing to realize that this aridity is actually the outcome of grace, the soul becomes plagued by the likelihood of having brought on this change by some personal fault or sin.

Merton vividly describes the ensuing inner struggle: "It is natural for one in this case to dread the loss of his faith, indeed of his own integrity and religious identity, and to cling desperately to whatever will seem to preserve the last shreds of belief. So he struggles, sometimes frantically, to recover a sense of comfort and conviction in formulated truths or familiar religious practices. His meditation becomes the scene of this *agonia*, this wrestling with nothingness and doubt. But the more he struggles the less comfort and assurance he has, and the more powerless he sees himself to be. Finally, he loses even the power to struggle. He feels himself ready to sink and drown in doubt and despair."[4]

This painful, agonizing questioning constitutes in fact a sign of authenticity of the night. Why? How?

It is precisely the presence of a burning desire to serve God in all fidelity that produces such intense spiritual anxiety about possibly not being in his service. If a person were insincere and not deeply searching for God, there would be no concern or solicitude regarding his/her commitment to God. Only the truly sincere are actually worried about their potential for insincerity. Only the truly faithful are in fact anxious about any taint of infidelity.

It is the actual presence of sincerity and fidelity that manifests the discrepancy between Christ and sin both living at the same time within the soul. There can never be peaceful coexistence between Love and selfishness, Life and death, Truth and falsehood. Therefore, were God not so intent upon transforming the soul into himself by participation, the soul would never experience the intensity of its innate resistance,

4CP, p. 99. See TS, p. 81.

its actual infidelity, its own insincerity: "When I act against my own will, that means that I have a self that acknowledges that the Law is good . . . . Oh, what a wretched man I am!" (Rm 7:16,24). St. Paul is but applying the gist of this "second sign," in all its down-to-earthness, to his own inner struggle.

"Hence, it is obvious that this dryness and inability to be satisfied do not result from laxity and tepidity, since a lukewarm person neither cares much nor has inward solicitude for the things of God."

This agonizing solicitude is further intensified by a heightened awareness that coexistent with a basic sincerity are elements of very real insincerity. This realization is not only one of possible sinfulness ("I could conceivably fall") but is rather the soul-wrenching experience of actual sinfulness ("I really am a sinner"). And the soul knows that this is no exaggeration: "Every single time I want to do good, something evil comes to hand" (Rm 7:21).

As God gradually and systematically removes the defense mechanisms which we so effectively used to avoid facing our insincere, false selves, we become in his light ever more aware of our lack of sincerity before God and each other as well as of our need for reconciliation.

The experience of the soul in this aspect of the night is very frequently and acutely that of getting worse. Instead of progressing spiritually, it has the impression and fear of regression. In reality, God is making significant progress with the soul, even though the soul's appraisal is quite the opposite due to the "newness of the exchange."[5] That is, up to this point the soul had been able to keep most of its actual sinfulness hidden

[5]*Night*, I, 9, 4.

behind rationalizations and defense mechanisms. But now that God has begun to remove these, the soul has no place to hide as before. Therefore, this ugliness, which had been below the surface, comes gushing forth into consciousness clammering to be seen for what it really is; namely, real insincerity, infidelity, sin.

Because this painful care and solicitude could also have its origin in sources other than the night of sense, a third sign and condition is necessary.

(3) "The third sign for the discernment of this purgation of sense is the powerlessness, in spite of one's efforts, to meditate or to make use of the imagination as was one's previous custom."

The third sign and condition consists in a radical change in one's praying habits. We now find that no matter how much effort we make at meditation, we are powerless to pray discursively as we did prior to this intense aridity.

In his introduction to this third sign, John describes the positive reality that causes the inability to meditate: This gift "is the beginning of a contemplation that is dark and dry to the senses. Ordinarily this contemplation, which is secret and hidden from the very one who receives it, imparts to the soul, together with the aridity and emptiness it effects in the senses, an inclination and desire to remain alone and in quietude."

Together with the inability to meditate, the soul is irresistibly drawn to seek out solitude in order to remain alone loving its Beloved. This positive thrust towards solitude as well as the aridity and the restless questioning are each the outcome of the "beginning of contemplation." In the perception of the soul receiving it, contemplation is "secret and hidden" not only by virtue of its elusive, spiritual quality, but also by virtue of the perplexing vicissitudes produced during the night.

This dark and arid contemplation is accompanied by a subtle spiritual delight, peace and joy. However, if the soul is concerned and solicitous for these spiritual benefits or if it tries to hang on to them, these delights dissipate immediately. Such is the degree of detachment and of sheer receptivity that is required of the soul in contemplation: "This interior refection is so delicate that ordinarily if the soul desires or tries to experience it, it cannot. For. . .this contemplation is active while the soul is most in leisure and carefreeness.[6] It is like air that escapes when one tries to grasp it in one's hand."

At times the presence or absence of these signs (regarding both the abandonment of discursive meditation and the authenticity of the sensory night) may be readily perceptible to the individual soul and/or to a competent spiritual director. Yet, more often than not the individual soul is more confused and reticent about applying these principles to itself than is an experienced director.

The transition from discursive meditation to contemplation may cover a considerable period of time and may tran-

[6]The Spanish text reads *en el mayor ocio y descuido* (*Night*, I, 9, 6). Peers translates it "most at ease and freest from care." Kavanaugh translates it "in idleness and unconcern." In our opinion Kavanaugh gives *ocio* and *descuido* a pejorative connotation that is not warranted by either the text or the context — "leisure" is not "idleness"; "carefreeness" is not "unconcern." See Thomas Merton, *Notes for a Philosophy of Solitude*, in *Disputed Questions* (Farrar, 1960), pp. 177-207.

spire in much ambivalence. It is difficult to discern whether the perplexing experience is truly the outcome of the beginning of contemplation or the result of laziness, personal faults or emotional disorders. In fact, the ambiguity can occasionally be so pronounced that neither a spiritual director nor the individual soul can immediately discern whether the soul is heading for a breakdown or for a breakthrough. While the night of contemplation and emotional disorders have nothing directly in common, certain symptoms that indicate emotional disturbances can nonetheless be mistaken for various aspects of the signs for discernment of contemplation and the dark night (and vice versa).

If what is undergone is truly from God, it will lead inevitably to an interior breakthrough. Since God's sole purpose in the contemplative night is to transform us in love and bring us to our full potential, he will never crush us or push us beyond our capacity to endure: "You can trust God not to let you be tried beyond your strength, and with any trial he will give you a way out of it and the strength to bear it" (1 Co 10:13).

However, if this emptiness, anxiety, propensity to be alone and the like stem from emotional disorders, then this experience can lead to introversion, withdrawal, lassitude and other pathological situations which hinder personality growth. "For when pure humor alone is the cause, everything ends in disgust and does harm to one's nature, and there are none of the desires to serve God which accompany purgative aridity." Yet, this is not to imply that God cannot use even a complete breakdown or insanity as an instrument of transformation and purification: "We know that by turning *everything* to their good, God cooperates with all those who love him" (Rm 8:28).

On the other hand, while the aridity, solicitude and non-discursiveness may be caused predominately by the contemplative night, one's discernment of its authenticity may be complicated by the presence of a host of immaturities and/or varying degrees of emotional and personality disorders. Generally in these instances God's purifying activity is not effectively hindered by these complications: "Even though the dryness may be furthered by melancholia or some other humor — as it often is — it does not thereby fail to produce its purgative effect in the appetite, for the soul will be deprived of every satisfaction and be concerned only with God."

It should be noted regarding both sets of signs (those in the preceding chapter as well as those in this chapter) that the absence of sin is not among these signs of authentic spiritual progress. To put it another way: the presence of very real sin in a person's life is not necessarily a counterindication of the presence of God's intense transforming activity within the soul, or of the soul's basically sincere response in love to his love. John of the Cross is too realistic to expect perfection at the beginning of contemplation. One cannot even expect perfection any time this side of the resurrection (see Ph 3:5-16; Rm 8:22-25), because each one of us — St. John of the Cross included — remains an actual sinner till death. No one gets through the night completely unscathed.

8

A Question

The following question is frequently asked: "When God leads a soul into the beginning of contemplation, does it ever again meditate discursively?"

Even when solitary prayer has become habitually contemplative, a rich, balanced life of prayer continues to embrace other prayer forms: the Eucharist, Divine Office, shared prayer and at times simplified discursive prayer. Yet, with the gift of contemplation, all prayer forms become increasingly permeated with a deeper contemplative thrust: that of loving receptivity.

In some instances when a soul becomes aware of its call to contemplation, it experiences an abrupt change in its praying habits. Discursive meditation is abandoned all at once. Usually in these cases contemplation has actually been in progress for some time, but without the soul consciously adverting to the fact. There may even have been an increasing realization that indeed something different was taking place in prayer, but instead of associating the change with deeper transformation, the soul may have been inclined to suspect regression.

More often, however, the transition from discursive meditation to contemplation is not so clear-cut, nor are the signs of authenticity all that easily discernible. The principles of discernment which we have been discussing are not a kind of checklist. Even though these principles are quite tersely formulated and universally applicable, the truths which they enunciate are uniquely translated into each soul's life according to all the singularity of God's call for that individual person.

Moreover, when the transition is prolonged, prayer may be sometimes discursive and sometimes contemplative from day to day or even within a given prayer period. "In the beginning, the habit of contemplation may not be so perfect that one can enter into it at will. Neither is it so remote from discursive meditation as to be incapable of it altogether. One can at times meditate . . . as before, and even discover something new in it. Indeed, at the outset of contemplation . . . the soul may still need to make use of meditation" from time to time.[1]

Often we begin to pray only to find that, at least for a while, we need to make some use of memory, intellect or will before being led into a more contemplative stance. A useful practice at such times is listening to a word, a phrase or a short verse from Scripture. Let God (through the word, phrase or verse) "work you over" at his own pace and in his own way. Then, when this simplified discursiveness has run its course, let it go and do not try to start up again with another passage. Thus,

---

[1]*Ascent*, II, 15, 1. See *Cloud*, 75.

you will be allowing yourself to be drawn more directly into the simplicity of loving surrender.

At other times, on beginning to pray the soul finds itself drawn immediately into loving and peaceful attentiveness towards God, without first engaging in even the most simplified discursive prayer.

Since in the beginning of contemplation the soul may sometimes contemplate and sometimes meditate, the practical question arises of how one is to know when it is appropriate no longer to pray discursively: "The indication will be that each time the soul sets out to meditate, it will instead find itself contemplating, and it will experience a lack of ability and desire to meditate discursively."[2]

In the transition from meditation to contemplation, a simple guideline to follow is this: pray as you *can* and not as you think you should.

If we approach prayer with fixed ideas of what our prayer should consist in, our deepest self will not be sufficiently open to the unexpected ways of God's grace. Rather we must follow the spontaneous and mysterious yearnings of the heart. When interiorly inclined to make acts of adoration, thanksgiving, petition, to reflect discursively about God or to ponder certain mysteries of salvation, we are to follow these inclinations wherever they may lead us. When drawn into a general, loving, peaceful awareness of God, we are to remain in this contemplative stance for however long the attraction lasts. If we pray as we can, whether we call it "discursive" or "contemplative," we will be responding to the true, inner promptings of the Spirit (see Rm 8:26-27). The need to pray sometimes

---

[2]*Ascent,* II, 15, 1.

discursively and sometimes contemplatively continues until contemplation becomes habitual.

Even when contemplation has become habitual, God may still occasionally move the soul during solitary prayer to reflect on certain particular considerations or to make some specific acts. When such a movement is from God, the soul must respond accordingly. (And when it arises spontaneously from within, one may assume that it is indeed from God.) For example, as a direct consequence of contemplation, a certain aspect of self-knowledge may break forth into consciousness. In order that God's will may be done within us, it may be necessary to meditate discursively on this fruit of contemplation.

Nevertheless, the soul must not delude itself into thinking that it is being moved by God to make discursive acts and considerations, when in fact it is being motivated by a subtle desire to escape the aridity of contemplation by "doing something useful." If we cling to some form of discursive activity — even the repetition of a single word — once an authentic movement from God has ceased, we only impede God's transforming activity and place an obstacle in the way of spiritual progress: "If the soul should desire to act on its own initiative, doing anything other than remaining in passive, loving attentiveness... *unless God should unite it to himself in some act*, it would impede the supernatural communication of God in loving contemplation."[3]

[3]*Flame*, 3, 34. The emphasis is our own. See *Ascent*, II, 12, 8.

9

Certain Difficulties

At the outset of contemplation the soul sometimes obstructs God's transforming activity by trying to cling to its former methods of prayer. Considering the dark and obscure ways of faith to be regression and craving for its former spiritual consolation and satisfaction, the soul behaves as did the Israelites in the desert: "When God began giving them the heavenly food which contained in itself all delight . . . they nonetheless felt a craving for the pleasures and satisfactions of the meats and onions they had eaten in Egypt. For their palates were accustomed and attracted to these rather than to the delicate . . . manna. So they wept and grieved for flesh-meat in the midst of this heavenly food."[1]

While God persists in keeping us in emptiness and interior silence, we persist in trying to initiate discursive activity

[1] *Night,* I, 9, 5. See Thomas Merton, *New Seeds of Contemplation* (New Directions, 1961), pp. 233-238.

despite the fact that the effort and the desire to do so is itself accompanied by a certain interior reluctance or even repugnance. St. John of the Cross describes this situation thus: "The soul resembles a child who, when his mother wants to carry him, kicks and cries in order to walk. He neither makes progress himself nor allows the mother to do so. Or the situation is like that of an artist trying to paint a portrait. If his subject keeps moving, the painter will be unable to accomplish anything at all, or the painting itself will be blurred."[2]

Furthermore, the interior agitation and fatigue caused by our efforts to retrieve the previous satisfaction of discursive prayer increase in proportion to the intensified resistance to our deeper desire to remain lovingly receptive: "The more they persist at discursive meditation the worse their state becomes, because they drag the soul further away from spiritual peace. They resemble one who has abandoned the greater for the lesser, or one who turns back on a road already covered and seeks to re-do what is already done."[3]

Only God himself can truly detach us from the desire to cling to our former ways of praying. He accomplishes this by impeding our efforts, leaving us in darkness and dryness, depriving us of our previous satisfaction, and not allowing us to make progress discursively no matter how hard we may try. He even makes the very effort we exert to pray in our own way a burden to us. Without our realizing what is happening, he breaks down our attachment and reveals our helplessness, our utter creatureliness, thereby teaching us to become ever

[2]*Flame*, 3, 66.

[3]*Ascent*, II, 12, 7. See *idem*, II, 14, 4; *Night*, I, 10, 1-2.

more abandoned in love and faith to the mystery of his everlasting mercy. Eventually, the outcome of our wrestling with God is submission in obedience to the unpredictable designs of his will. We humbly stand before him as did Jeremiah and proclaim: "You have opened me wide, Yahweh, and I have let myself be opened. You have overpowered me. You were the stronger" (Jr 20:7).

Nevertheless, even when we follow the deeper desire to remain loving our Beloved, many thoughts arise that disquiet us and make us think that we are being led far away from the contemplation we had so hoped to receive. Because of the absence of the particular and the concrete, we easily become overly concerned that we are wasting time, that we are doing nothing. Further scruples arise suggesting that laziness must be the cause of this inability to discourse, that we should try even more diligently to meditate as before.

Since it can no longer do or think anything "useful" in prayer, the soul wonders whether it would not be more profitable to abandon this "prayer" altogether in order to read, to make preparations related to ministry, to perform some charitable work — just anything other than persist in this scattered emptiness. Although our deepest self abides in a peaceful, loving attentiveness towards God, on a conscious level we may experience a veritable irksomeness at the prospect of remaining in the obscurity of faith. Occasionally too, this weariness may even lead the soul to be repelled by the very thought of spending time in solitary prayer. This in turn causes it further distress since the soul so deeply desires to love God and remain in his love.

No matter how convincing these temptations may seem,

the soul must persevere patiently in prayer, being content to abide in loving attentiveness in God without trying to force itself to say, to do or to think anything. God now desires that the soul let go all concern, all effort and all desire to experience something of him in a sensory manner. Of course, should some consolation occur from within, we naturally let it come forth. But we must not attempt to produce such sensory satisfaction by our initiative: "The attitude necessary in this night of sense is to pay no attention to discursive meditation, since this is not the time for it. They should rather allow the soul to remain in rest and quietude, although it may seem clear to them that they are doing nothing and are wasting their time, and even though they believe that this disinclination to think of anything is due to their own laxity. The truth is that they will be doing quite sufficient, if they just have patience and persevere in prayer, without making any effort."[4]

Yes, just "have patience and persevere in prayer without making any effort..." "Effort," of course, in the sense of "trying to try," "trying to do something, anything." There is no effort imaginable that is more demanding than the "non-effort" just to remain being loved and loving. The effort that is required "to make no effort" in order to remain open and receptive is the most disciplined and exigent effort of all.

Yes, just "persevere in prayer." This is not only good advice, but also a most important principle of discernment regarding the authenticity of one's prayer. For the ability to persevere in remaining being loved and loving, day after day, week after week, year after year — in painful, perplexing aridity — can come only from God. No human will is stubborn enough to

[4]*Night*, I, 10, 4. See *Flame*, 3, 33; *Ascent*, II, 12, 8; *Cloud*, 68-69; *PC*, 3.

simply go through these motions. If the endurance is from you, you will inevitably abandon it. If the perseverance is from God, you can never effectively abandon prayer indefinitely, for "the One who has begun this good work in you will bring it to completion" (Ph 1:6; see Ph 1:11; Rm 11:29; Is 55:10-11).

In all this aridity, further questions arise: How is God transforming me? Since I don't feel love for him, do I really love him? What in the world am I doing here?

While such questions are in themselves normal, we must not become preoccupied with seeking specific answers to them. The insistence on knowing these answers with certitude leads only to unnecessary introspection and preoccupation with self. Then, instead of remaining lovingly attentive in God, we become centered on some-thing: our *self*. The result of such egocentricity is the loss of interior peace and quietude. Rather than seeking answers to these questions, we must be content to undergo the questioning itself, maintaining a spirit of inner tranquility in the midst of the turmoil: "Let them suffer these scruples and remain at peace, since there is no question save of their being at ease and having freedom of spirit."[5]

When God begins to lead a soul into contemplation, a certain amount of discouragement and confusion is not only normal but salvific as well. However, as beginners we often lose sight of just how normal and salvific this condition really is. We become perplexed and distraught over the constant presence of inner struggle and our attentiveness becomes fixed on the struggle itself. This preoccupation serves only to further intensify the suffering which in turn makes us even more

[5]*Night*, I, 10, 5. "The contemplative is one who would rather not know than know. . . . Rather not have *proof* that God loves him" (CP, p. 89).

centered upon self. Caught in this circle, we tend to become progressively more discouraged at our discouragement, more confused at our confusion. The only way out of this ensnarement is more realistic-trust in God who is ever with us guiding us safely and securely through the night. He rescues us from this whirlwind of undue perplexity and discouragement by teaching us that all we must do is persevere peacefully and remain attentive to him in love, faith and hope.

Since contemplation transpires in our innermost being where God dwells secretly and hiddenly, the quality of our prayer cannot be judged by any of our usual conscious perceptions. Nevertheless, we are frequently inclined to judge the quality of prayer by its surface accompaniments. If we receive a meaningful insight or some sensible feeling of peace or of the presence of God, we tend to consider such tangible consolation as indicative of deep communion with him. On the other hand, the experience of aridity, desolation or temptation during prayer leads us to conclude that we either have not been present to God at all or at best only superficially. Human standards of judgment cannot be applied in this manner to appraise the wholly mysterious and unpredictable ways of God. For, "my thoughts are not your thoughts. My ways are not your ways — it is Yahweh who speaks" (Is 55:8-9).

Deep transformation may transpire in what we might term tranquil prayer and little transformation may occur in what we might experience as more difficult prayer. However, it may also be that the prayer in which God is most effectively operative is precisely that which we judge to be of least or of no value. And the prayer we consider to be of greatest value in reality may lack much quality and depth. While our conscious, surface experience in prayer is not totally unrelated to

God's transforming activity within, it nevertheless cannot furnish authentic indications as to the actual intensity of God's true presence: "Neither is the sublime communication nor the sensible awareness of his nearness a sure testimony of His gracious presence, nor is dryness and the lack of these a sure testimony of his absence."[6]

It is not unusual, from day to day and even within a given period of prayer, for our experience of contemplation to vary from consolation to aridity, from the peace-filling awareness of the presence of God to the perplexing sense of his apparent absence. Over a period of time a person may run the entire gamut of emotional possibilities during contemplative prayer: from fear to ease, from tension to joy, from a sense of despair to a feeling of love, from utter "blah" to spontaneous orgasm. Quite literally anything can happen during deep contemplation, and it often occurs without any definable rhyme or reason. Each of these surface, emotional reactions is related to whatever it is that God is doing in the depths of the soul in love. But the soul can never make the specific link with exactly what he is doing. Nor should the soul even try to establish such a causal relationship. Rather it should simply suffer, endure all these emotional reactions, keeping its loving attentiveness on God alone.

Nevertheless, the predominant emotional reaction during prayer — especially at the beginning of contemplation — is one of a general, nondescript emptiness. This situation may last for a long time: years, even decades in some instances. Yet, while this emptiness is particularly disquieting at the outset, the soul does gradually learn to be at home with it, until it

[6]*Canticle,* I, 3.

actually "acquiesces in the unknown and peacefully advances where it does not see the way."[7]

Whatever its experience, the soul must persevere in solitary prayer. This is essential for growth in Christ.

Needless to say, a spiritual director can be an invaluable instrument that God often uses to help dispel the many illusions in one's prayer life. A competent director can do much to assist a soul through the turmoil and darkness of this night to a greater awareness of the mystery of God's transforming love. A director guides and encourages the soul to become more at home in unknowing, to be content to acquiesce in the darkness of faith and to learn to cope maturely with difficulties.

When the opportunity for spiritual guidance is available, we sometimes find that we are neither able nor do we know how to describe our prayer in precise terms. When our director asks us how we pray, we may feel embarrassed at having nothing to relate. We stammer and search for a way to express the inexpressible. We find only vague, general words to describe our deepest experiences. Often the most that can be said is that while we are confused and appear to be doing nothing, there is a vague sense of meaningfulness in simply remaining in love during prayer.

We must learn to be comfortable with being unable to pin down precisely what is transpiring. The inability to describe our prayer in concrete, specific terms may itself be a sign of authenticity. Because contemplation is always beyond the tangible and perceptible, it cannot be reduced to clear-cut categories: "Since the wisdom of this contemplation is the

[7]CP, p. 94.

language of God to the soul, addressed by Pure Spirit to pure spirit, anything that is less than spirit, such as the senses, cannot perceive it. Thus this wisdom is secret to the senses. They have neither the knowledge nor the ability to speak of it, nor do they even desire to do so, because it is beyond words."[8]

If we are in need of guidance and God does not provide us with a spiritual director, we may be confident that he will most certainly provide the necessary direction through some other means: for instance, daily events, homilies, spiritual reading, persons we encounter. All we need is the openness of heart to recognize the signs as they are given through his loving providence.

[8]*Night*, II, 17, 4. See *Canticle*, 7, 10.

10

Storms and Trials of Sense

A special difficulty in the night of contemplation is the frequent bombardment of the soul by what St. John of the Cross calls "trials of sense."[1] While the soul deeply desires to remain receptive to God, it experiences nonetheless the allurement of certain sinful tendencies. Strong and vehement temptations often assail the soul even in prayer, causing it to question how it could possibly be communing in any way with God.

John of the Cross, on the basis of his own personal experience of the night as well as his experience as spiritual director, synthesizes what he considers the three most fre-

---

[1]*Night*, I, 14, 1-6. The same reference holds true for all the quoted passages in this chapter, unless otherwise identified. See *Flame*, 2, 24-30.

quent trials which ordinarily accompany the night of sense. They are: (1) the "spirit of fornication," (2) the "spirit of blasphemy" and (3) the "spirit of dizziness."

(1) The first trial of the night of sense occurs for some souls when "the angel of Satan, which is the spirit of fornication, is given to them in order to buffet their senses with abominable and strong temptations and to afflict them with foul thoughts and very vivid images. This is sometimes a worse affliction for them than death."[2]

This spirit of fornication may include sexual fantasizing, wanderings of the imagination, involuntary genital movements, the temptation to autoeroticism, an inordinate desire for sexual intercourse or preoccupation with genital intimacies. This spirit may also be manifested in a variety of tendencies ranging from vanity and machismo to excessive eating and drinking.

The spirit of fornication arises out of a deep-rooted selfishness within the soul: the craving to *feel* pleasure. The concupiscible appetite becomes frenzied in its confusion and lack of satisfaction which result directly from the intense aridity of the night. Thus, the concupiscible aspect of the human person frantically seeks consolation — any sensory compensation —wherever it can find it. Depending on a wide range of circumstances and personality traits, this craving for a compensatory feeling can concretize itself in any excessive manifestation of the concupiscible order.

---

[2]John is obviously borrowing some of his phraseology from St. Paul: "There was given to me a thorn in the flesh, an angel of Satan, in order to buffet me..." (2 Co 12:7). The term "spirit of fornication" (*ruah wenunim*) is used in Ho 4:12; 5:4.

(2) "At other times in this night the spirit of blasphemy is added. It mingles intolerable blasphemies with all their ideas and thoughts. At times these are so forcefully suggested to the imagination that it almost makes these souls pronounce them. This causes them grave torment."

This spirit includes various temptations deriving from the irascible appetite. The soul may be inclined to blame God for letting the confusion and the aridity happen. This in turn can easily lead to feelings of anger or resentment towards him. Losing sight of the positive value of the night, the soul may question: "Why is God punishing me?" "How can he be so cruel?" The soul may agonize over why God seems so weak and powerless to help in this hour of such need: "He saved others" (Mt 27:42); "why can't he help me right now the way I want?" The soul may even be tempted to wonder whether a personal, loving God exists at all.

At other times the soul may become extremely annoyed at God's apparent slowness in transforming it. It may even be so presumptuous as to attempt to control God by demanding that he immediately resolve all its difficulties, or at least that he give it some tangible sign that he is present: "If you are really God's Son, come down from the cross" (Mt 27:40).

As with the previous spirit, this one also arises from a deep-rooted selfishness within the soul: the craving to *be in control* (especially of one's own destiny). Its irascible appetite becomes so distraught over the persistent lack of any sensory relief from the aridity of the night that it strikes out in frustration at whatever it can hit. In this condition, it is not unusual to misappropriate one's anger: for example, the wife who tears into her husband (when she is really upset with

God); or the priest who takes it out on a parishioner (when he is actually very frustrated with having to admit the frightening extent of his own inner poverty). The soul often has the impression in this night that it is more irritable and impatient than ever before.

(3) "At still other times another abominable spirit, which Isaias calls *spiritum vertiginis* (19:14),[3] is given to them, not for their downfall but to exercise them. This spirit darkens their senses in such a way that it fills them with a thousand scruples and perplexities so intricate to their judgment that they can never satisfy themselves with anything, or find support for their judgment in any advice or idea."

When this spirit of dizziness strikes, it leaves the soul reeling in a whirlwind of terrifying uncertainty. Intense spiritual anxiety grips it, hounding it with thoughts that possibly it is not serving God, that it may be perverse beyond redemption. However much searching the soul attempts at this time, it cannot come to any peaceful resolution as to what God's will actually is or whether it is even letting his will be done. In discerning the authenticity of its prayer, for example, the matter may seem so complex and intricate that it is left in utter confusion for weeks, months, years. Even when a spiritual director confirms the apparent authenticity of its prayer, or gives advice on how to proceed appropriately, the soul cannot be content with this counsel as long as this spirit persists. In fact, such advice sometimes leaves it all the more perplexed.

[3]John is quoting the *Vulgate*: "spirit of dizziness (vertigo)." The Hebrew text reads *ruah iweim*: literally, "the spirit of overturning (of ruin, overthrowing, perversity.)"

The spirit of dizziness is frequently most acute in making fundamental options, in discerning calls within a call, in resolving crises regarding the spiritualization of personal relationships. "This particular trial is one of the severest goads and horrors of this night, very closely akin to that which occurs in the other night."

This spirit arises from an even deeper-rooted selfishness than the previous two: the insatiable need for reassurance and the craving *to know*. As the concupiscible and irascible appetites are in themselves positive forces within the human person, so the normal need for affirmation and knowledge is of itself a constructive drive within the soul. However, when the soul experiences a self-centered craving to know which in effect contradicts the "unknowing" required by the depths of mystery to which it is being drawn, then there is deep interior turmoil. The same for reassurance: when the soul's need for tangible affirmation begins to contradict the limitless demands of true faith and trust in God, then its experiences of the night can reach unimaginable intensity.

All the while the soul is experiencing uncontrollable urges to feel, to dominate and to know it is receiving very subtle and mysterious joy, peace and wisdom. But due to the force of these storms and the intensity of the attachment to self, it is usually a long time before the purified soul can appreciate what it has been receiving all along.

Each of these storms is presented by John in the passive voice: "the spirit of fornication is given...", "the spirit of blasphemy is added...", "the spirit of dizziness is given...." This indicates that they happen to the soul at the initiative of another.

John of the Cross teaches that God himself is their author. These are God's own "spiritual exercises" — infinitely more spiritualizing and exercising than any of the spiritual exercises of the classical ascetical masters, "God ordinarily sends these storms and trials in this night of sense to those whom he intends to put in the other night," that of spirit. "Thus, having been chastened and buffeted, these souls may be exercised and disposed . . . for the union of Wisdom which will be granted to them there."

John's theology but reflects the teaching of Scripture on this point: "Jesus was sent by the Spirit out into the wilderness in order to be tempted" (Mt 4:1). "There was given to me a thorn in the flesh, an angel of Satan in order to buffet me and stop me from getting too proud" (2 Co 12:7). "Because you were acceptable to God, it was necessary that temptation prove you" (Tb 12:13).

What then is the relationship of such temptations to God's transforming activity? Does the expression, "God sends these storms and trials," imply that God wills that we be tempted? If so, in what sense?

The classical expression of the relationship between God and evil may be synthesized thus: God wills good directly. God wills physical evil indirectly. God only permits moral evil. While this formula is true as far as it goes, it nevertheless does not do justice to the enigmatic truth that John of the Cross and the above scriptural passages are attempting to reveal.

Any event or situation, rather than being entirely good or entirely evil, contains intermingled elements of both good and evil, virtue and sin, maturity and selfishness. We respond in each instance by fostering the good and at the same time by resisting the evil. Moreover, both good and evil live in each one of us. In my deepest self, "I live no longer I, but Christ lives in me" (Ga 2:20). And , at the very same time, on a behavioral level, I am also the slave of "sin living in me" (Rm 7:17).

The coexistence of sincerity and selfishness is manifest throughout our whole being — in our every action, attitude, intention and desire. However selfless our motives may be in any given situation, our selfishness is also operative to some extent: "In fact, this seems to be the rule: Every single time I want to do good, something evil comes to hand. In my innermost self, I dearly love God's law, but I see my body follows a different law that battles against the law my reason dictates" (Rm 7:21-22). It becomes a question then of whether in any particular act we are motivated predominately by God living in us, or by sin living in us.

In contemplation the struggle between God in us and sin in us is given unparalleled vent. The consciousness — indeed, the all-embracing experience — of personal sinfulness that results from contemplation is indescribably more acute and existential than any that discursive examination of conscience, whether "particular" or "general," could ever produce. As God wells up within the soul, everything that cannot be divinized is agitated, breaks loose and comes gushing forth into consciousness. In Christ, our deep-seated weaknesses and imperfections are gradually and systematically uprooted. We feel this wrenching in every fibre of our being.

In contemplation "there arises within the soul contraries against contraries — the things of the soul versus the things of God which assail the soul. . . . Herein these contraries react one against the other, making war in the soul, trying to expel each other in order to reign supreme. In other words, the virtues and properties of God, which are perfect in the extreme, war against the habits and properties of the soul, which are imperfect in the extreme. Thus the soul has to suffer these two contraries within itself."[4]

Consider this analogy. Suppose you return to the attic of your childhood home, an attic no one has set foot in for many years. You stand there peering through the glass of the door at the attic entrance. Everything inside appears so very orderly and peaceful: old rockers, beds, family portraits draped in sheets. Then you open the door and step inside. Even before you are halfway across the room you are almost suffocating from dust coming from everywhere: off the floor, off the walls, off the ceiling.

What on earth happened? Before you entered, everything seemed so serene. Yet in reality that dust was present all the while, even though you could not see it. On entering, the mere movement of your body agitated everything. So too with regard to the soul: You may *think* that everything deep inside is well in order, but let God start moving within your soul and see if he does not stir up a veritable hornet's nest. His transforming activity will force into your consciousness an ever greater awareness of the real selfishness and duplicity that has always been unconsciously operative in all your behavior. (And if you do not really believe that you have always been this way, just ask someone who has had to live with you! Possibly others have been trying to tell you for years what you are only now beginning to discover.)

[4]*Flame*, I, 22. See Augustine, *Tract. in Joh.* 41, 10.

Obviously the expression, "God sends these storms," does not imply that these trials of sense come from God as such. Rather, it means that the temptations arise from the soul having come into direct contact with God's transforming love. "The darkness and other evils which the soul experiences as the divine light assails it are not caused by the light. On the contrary, they proceed from the soul itself, and the light illumines the soul so that it may see them."[5]

St. James affirms the same basic truth in this manner: "Never, when you have been tempted, say, 'God sent the temptation.' God cannot be tempted to do anything wrong, and he does not tempt anybody. Everybody who is tempted is attracted and seduced by his own wrong desire" (Jm 1:13-14). These storms come then from us: from "sin living in me" (Rm 7:17).

John of the Cross refers to these trials of sense as "storms" rather than "distractions." The term "distraction" may be appropriate in the context of discursive meditation, since it implies that our attention is drawn away from a particular trend of thought by someone or something else. However, in contemplation where the soul is lovingly attentive to God without any particular trend of thought, the word "storm" is a far more accurate description of the turbulence which ensues from the soul's encounter with its Beloved.

Although something of the spirit of fornication, the spirit of dizziness and the spirit of blasphemy is ordinarily undergone by everyone in the night of sense, each soul experiences these storms in a way and to an intensity that is uniquely personal. The length of time that an individual is kept in this "fast and

[5]*Night*, II, 13, 10. See *idem*, II, 5, 5-7; II, 9, 11; II, 10, 2-4; II, 16, 11.

penance of sense" cannot be predicted, since it depends on the depth of transformation in love which God desires for the person, the extent of purification necessary, and one's capacity and strength to endure suffering. Those who have the capacity and strength to suffer more deeply, God purges more quickly and intensely. Others who are unable to sustain constant, intense suffering, he purges more slowly, usually furnishing them with occasional consolations to encourage them. Yet, however quickly God may transform us, generally we all must endure these storms for a long time.

At times a soul may respond that it is conscious of one or other of these storms, but not all three. Or else, that some of them are quite intense, while one or other is practically negligible. John of the Cross is saying that everyone encounters in this night increased difficulties arising from one's *concupiscible* and *irascible* appetites as well as from *inner confusion* of judgment and emotions — some more, some less. However, some souls do not recognize the technical terms that spiritual directors or authors use to describe these storms and therefore do not associate the terminology with what they are in fact experiencing. Others may see their inner struggle as so normal an outgrowth of maturing that they do not consider these as unusually difficult and therefore would not really call them "storms." Or, at a given moment it may be that in reality the soul has not yet experienced all three, but it will experience each one sooner or later, one way or another, more or less.

In itself the bombardment of our senses by these storms does not negatively affect the quality of contemplative prayer. It is precisely because God's transforming love is purifying us that the awareness of personal sin is given such vehement expression in our consciousness. These storms are the normal outcome of a sinner coming into direct and immediate contact with God himself. Furthermore, contemplation transpires in our innermost being while these storms rage on the periphery of our person.

Although these storms do not of themselves adversely affect our prayer, we can nevertheless obstruct God's activity by not conducting ourselves properly when they arise. Instead of being overly solicitous and preoccupied with them (or with self suffering them), we must remain in interior tranquility, without either fighting them or giving in to them. We must endure them.

That is a difficult truth. It is difficult for some to understand and difficult for all to put into practice. Quite obviously the soul cannot give in to these storms without obstructing God's grace. This would be to succumb to temptation. Nor can the soul directly fight them either. They are too formidable and arise from too deep within to be dealt with effectively in a direct manner. If the soul does try to fight these storms, one of two things will almost inevitably result: either the soul will give in to them (usually out of frustration) or it will repress them (usually out of desperation). And we all know that what is repressed eventually recurs, even more strongly. Thus the only truly humanizing and spiritualizing way to cope with this kind of onslaught is *padecer*[6]: suffer them, endure them. Just let yourself humbly experience them as well as your own inner poverty with them, and undergo with

[6]This is the Spanish term that John of the Cross employs consistently both as a verb and as a noun in this and similar contexts.

gentleness the temptations that befall you, until they have run their course.

Either to fight these storms or to give in to them is to take one's attentiveness away from God and to fix it on some-thing: the storming itself or self being stormed. All that God asks is that we peacefully undergo the trials of sense, keeping our attentiveness riveted on him in love.

These storms are both good and evil. They are evil in the sense that they are painful onslaughts of the sin and weakness truly living within us. But at the same time they also have a most positive function in the process of our transformation in that they are the spiritual exercises which God uses to purge our egocentricity. In using these trials of sense as instruments to awaken us to the depths of our poverty and helplessness, God thereby lures us to a more radical abandonment to himself in love.

11

An Area of Conflict

Some physical solitude is necessary for growth in prayer. Yet, it sometimes happens that a person feels called to more external solitude than the concrete circumstances of one's vocation normally would permit.

By virtue of the universal call to holiness all persons are called to deeper and deeper interior solitude regardless of their ministry, apostolate, vocation or job (social workers as well as hermits, housewives as well as nuns). What we are treating in this chapter, however, is rather a possible call by God to greater and greater physical (exterior) solitude. While everyone is called to contemplative prayer, authentic contemplative vocations (as a way of life) are quite rare. Although a call to deeper solitude is not synonymous with "contemplative vocation," it nevertheless is a call which accentuates the contemplative dimension in life. Therefore it must be carefully discerned lest the soul drift into ever greater isolation.

The phrase "more physical (external) solitude" can be expressive of anything from living alone in an apartment to being dispensed from certain communal exercises in view of more solitary prayer — anything from taking more time off and more leisure to a substantial reduction in workload and ministerial responsibility in view of a more solitary life.

The principles which follow are formulated particularly with priests, brothers and sisters in mind, since their situations usually cause more complications in this matter, due to responsibilities which obedience and community necessarily elicit in their lives and in their decision-making processes. However, *mutatis mutandis* these same principles are equally applicable to any person, regardless of one's specific calling in life.

Since all that we shall be discussing in this chapter will be taking place in a context which diametrically opposes *solitude* and *isolation*, let us briefly explain something of what we mean by each term. We distinguish isolation from true solitude like two entities as opposed to each other as light and darkness.

In the context of contemplation, isolation denotes a force that can drive you out of your mind. It is closing in upon oneself, sheer selfishness, regression into self-pity, self-complacency. It is the shunning of others and of personal responsibility in order to keep the true light out. Usually loneliness (the feeling of being cut off) and boredom (overindulgence in the created) are characteristic symptoms of isolation.

On the other hand, solitude denotes a force that will drive you into becoming fully who you are to become. It is the being drawn into self by God so that he may empty self of selfishness. Solitude is the basis of all personalism and altruism: If you are not at home with yourself, you will never be at home with anyone else. Solitude is risk, leap forward into the Other. It is being alone in order to let the full light in. Aloneness (being alone with God) and aridity (the emptiness one experiences when the created, finite heart is being opened to uncreated, infinite Love) are characteristic accompaniments of true solitude.

Now, when a person believes himself/herself called to more external solitude than the concrete circumstances of his/her vocation (state in life) normally would permit, one of two situations arises. *Either*, after careful discernment with one's spiritual guides, the possible authenticity of this call is positively indicated. *Or*, in discerning the possible authenticity of its desire, the soul meets with serious reservations or outright contradiction from its spiritual guides.

In the *first instance*, the soul may proceed in the direction of greater solitude with support and encouragement. But careful ongoing discernment, according to the principles enunciated below (especially in *Part I, Groups B & C*), must accompany the soul into solitude. Particularly with regard to the *second instance* — where there is conflict in discernment — we offer the following pastoral guidelines and procedures.

Part I — In the context of proportionate mutual sincerity:

In presenting the following three groups of principles we assume, in either of the above instances, that all the parties involved in the discernment are each searching for God's will with proportionate sincerity and truth.

Group A

How is the soul to proceed, when the desire for more physical solitude conflicts with the discernment of one's spiritual director (this may also include: confessor, confidant, spiritual advisor) and/or one's legitimate authority (this may include: religious superior, moderator, community)?

First of all, while the conflict lasts, the soul should refrain from making any definitive change of lifestyle and continue searching for God's will, together with the others involved, by following the same road that has brought it to this threshold of discernment: "If there is some point on which you see things differently, God will make it clear to you" eventually, somehow. "Meanwhile, let us go forward on the same road that has brought us to where we are" (Ph 3:15-16).

God normally bestows a spiritual gift in the raw, requiring much time, sweat and tears for its development. Furthermore, it frequently happens that what God ultimately intends for the soul is not envisaged by any of the parties involved at the outset of the discernment process. Sometimes too, what God is actually drawing the soul towards does not even exist as a viable possibility until much later in the discernment (that is, after many blind alleys, contradictions and failures).

A *second suggestion* for resolving the conflict is to seek the advice of a neutral party (someone other than one's spiritual director and legitimate authority). This person must be truly competent as well as impartial. Furthermore, this neutral party must be given all the facts in the situation. That is, all the divergent points of view together with their respective contexts must be discussed. Moreover, the soul must not be so naive as to think that all this can be accomplished in just one or two sittings. And even after all this painstaking consultation, serious questions as to the authenticity of the soul's desire may still persist.

A *third suggestion* is that the soul be allowed to discern the possible authenticity of its desire for greater solitude by actually testing the desire for a prolonged period (six months, a year) in a contemplative setting: for example, in a house of prayer, a monastery or in some out-of-the-way place. In such an instance, competent, ongoing spiritual direction would be essential.

A *fourth suggestion* is this: In the event that the implementation of the previous three suggestions fails to resolve the conflict, the soul should submit in obedient faith to the sincere discernment of its spiritual director and legitimate authority. In this act of submitting, the soul should allow its quest for greater solitude to mature, seek a more spiritualized expression of it, and go on about the Father's business.

Group B

In either case — when the soul's desire for greater solitude is accompanied by positive signs or when conflicting interpretations arise in the discernment — continuing discernment is always necessary. The following five points should receive much prayerful attention:

(1) *The quality of one's present interior and exterior solitude:* Is the thrust of my solitude really towards inner freedom, creativity and spontaneity, or do I bind myself by self-imposed routines and structures? Am I drawn to be alone because I am called to be alone with God or because I enjoy being alone

with myself thereby being spared certain inconveniences and responsibilities that arise from living with others? Is there an inner discipline in the way I live out solitude, or am I prone to laziness and daydreaming?

(2) *The quality of one's study*: Concomitant with my desire "to be," is there also an inner need to actively search into the mysteries of salvation through serious study? Lack of consistency and perseverance in difficult study may be indicative of a deeply complacent desire for unchallenged ease and a comfortable existence. Complacency of any sort is diametrically opposed to true solitude. How do I study? Is there a receptive thrust to my study, or am I unduly structured in my pursuit of deeper truth? Do I exhibit a know-it-all attitude? Do I tense up when confronted with ideas and approaches which challenge my own preconceptions and attitudes?

(3) *The quality of one's activity*: Is there harmony and integration between prayer and activity in my life? Or is what I consider a call to solitude arising from a dichotomy between prayer and activity? Is solitude being sought as a way out of unnecessary busyness or frantic activity of my own making? Is activity itself a form of praying, or do I see it as something apart from prayer.[1]

(4) *The ability to change with change*: Am I open to let life happen as God wants it to happen, or do I tend to rigidly adhere to my own predetermined ways? When God chooses to send people, situations into my life — just when I had planned to be alone — do I maintain an attitude of listening in all that comes my way, or do I become interiorly scattered and agitated? In discerning the possible call to more exterior

[1]See *DM*, pp.70-73 *Detachment through Action.*

solitude, am I really willing to let go what I think to be the "answer"? Do I allow my will to be modified by the challenge which God reveals through my director, religious superior and/or community?

(5) *The ability to wait with patience:* "Since we are not saved yet, we must hope to be saved — it is something we must wait for with patience" (Rm 8:25). Am I willing to acquiesce in the unknown and wait patiently, letting God bring me where he desires me to be? Or am I demanding an answer before its time? Am I insisting that my way be his way?

We might add a kind of "sixth point": namely, how clearly and how surely does the soul respond to the questions raised in the previous "five points"? If the soul approaches the above questions as one would a questionnaire and scores oneself quite highly, such certitude regarding one's spiritual progress and such clarity in knowing one's true self may well be a sign of deep-rooted pride, complacency and/or illusion. Such a soul may not be seeking solitude at all, but out-and-out isolation.

Group C

In seeking more physical solitude, a person should be particularly alert to certain danger signs. The presence of one or other of these signs does not necessarily indicate the absence of a call to greater solitude, for frequently something of these tendencies persists even when an authentic call is discerned. Yet, evidence of these signs does raise serious questions which must be honestly faced. Prayerful attention should be especially given to whether the predominant tendency is towards solitude or towards isolation, and whether greater physical solitude is truly advisable under the circumstances. These danger signs are:

(1) *Fixation on what the soul considers an "ideal" solitary place or living situation:* Such a fixation often arises from the mistaken belief that what the soul considers "ideal" would in fact offer an easier, safer, better way to God than does one's immediate living situation. At times such a fixation stems from the illusion that a milieu free of certain trying difficulties would be more conducive to one's growth. In such instances it frequently is not solitude that is being sought, but rather escape from reality, responsibility or challenge. Generally, the fixation manifests itself by a person's claim to certainty that God is calling one to a particular place or situation regardless of what anyone else thinks. Moreover this claim is often defended by an elaborate system of reasoning that has a pat answer to every objection which the director or legitimate authority may pose. This kind of fixation can exist for a long time in a soul who may be otherwise quite sincere and discerning.

(2) *Withdrawal:* Sometimes what a person believes is a call to greater exterior solitude may in fact be a propensity to cut oneself off from God and from his world. It may be nothing more than an attempt to safeguard illusion. To seek physical aloneness because of feelings of rejection, a sense of failure or an inability to cope with tensions, conflicts or persons is a very misguided and potentially self-destructive venture. The prayer of the isolationist is: "Just leave me alone!"

(3) *Personality disorders:* Intense, prolonged exterior solitude may not be advisable for a person in whom pronounced

personality disorders or psychotic tendencies are detected. Too much aloneness may prove detrimental, since it may not provide the person with necessary outlets (e.g., more direct interaction with others, certain types of diversion) for learning to cope more maturely with these weaknesses. However, limited solitude, especially when accompanied by competent spiritual direction, may be helpful in some instances. There are times too when God may indeed call a soul to a limited period of exterior solitude in order to bring it to a better consciousness of its emotional disorder and/or to deepen its faith. Such an instance would usually occur only after the soul has reached a basic maturity and can deal constructively with its deficiencies.

The above three groups of principles could also be helpful in discerning a strictly contemplative or an eremitical vocation. However, discernment of such vocations is much more intricate than what is presented in this chapter and would require the consideration of certain other factors (e.g., the leaving of one's present way of life to embrace a radically different one).

Part II — In the context where the soul lacks sufficient sincerity:

In all that we have considered up to this point, we have assumed that the person in question, the spiritual director and legitimate authority are each seeking God's will with proportionate sincerity. That is, all parties involved are honestly doing the best they can, given the normal limitations of a discernment process. What procedure then might be suggested when the director and/or legitimate authority become convinced that the soul is not so sincerely and openly searching for God's will?

Basically, either of two approaches may be advisable.

First, the director or superior can stand firmly by his/her discernment and insist that the soul submit to this guidance in a spirit of obedience. If the soul does submit in humble faith, God will surely bring forth much good through obedience to one's spiritual guides. If the soul refuses to submit in obedience, the spiritual director and/or legitimate authority must not give in to the soul's obstinacy or manipulation, even if this means severing the relationship with the person in question.

A *second* alternative is open to the spiritual director and/or legitimate authority: namely, they may allow the soul to go its own way in order to discover for itself what is and what is not of God in its persistent demands. Thus, they would be simply applying the advice of Gamaliel: "Leave these men alone and let them go on . . . . For if this purpose or work of theirs is of human origin, it will break up of its own accord. But if it does in fact come from God, you will not only be unable to turn them from their design, but you might even find yourselves fighting against God" (Acts 5:38-39).

There are two profound truths of human behavior couched in this advice of Gamaliel: *on the one hand*, the principal way most people (if not all) really learn is by making their own mistakes, learning their own lessons. Remember the headstrong son of the "Prodigal Father" (Lk 15:11-32). And like that same Father, the spiritual guides of the soul must be lovingly ready to pick up the pieces once the soul has come to its senses. *On the other hand*, God's thoughts are not our thoughts (Is 55:8-9). Thus, not only may the soul in question not be perceiving God's will all that well, but also what God really wills may be quite other than what both the spiritual director and one's legitimate authority envisage at a given point in the discernment process.

Needless to say, consultation with persons likely to be able to furnish insight (for example: a psychologist or psychiatrist, someone actually living a solitary contemplative life, a close friend of the person in question) would be most helpful in determining which of these two basic approaches to take. Consultation can likewise assist in determining which modalities to introduce into the approach that is finally chosen.

Part III — In the context where the soul's spiritual guides lack sufficient sincerity:

The soul seeking greater physical solitude may become convinced that its director and/or superior is not seeking God's will in the situation with proportionate sincerity. How might the soul proceed under these circumstances?

First of all, the soul must be very careful not to presume insincerity or to project it upon others, especially in heated arguments and vehement confrontations. The soul can abuse "what-I-feel" just as easily as a superior can abuse authority. Moreover, far more persons have authority problems than are generally aware that they do. Therefore the soul must explore quite thoroughly these very real possibilities.

Secondly, the soul must be tolerant of the human weaknesses inherent in any situation of conflict — weaknesses within each person involved (the soul included). We all have our own ideas, experiences, fears, immaturities, dependencies, biases, ways. Usually, however, the most irksome situations in regard to one's superior are those which involve money and/or which the soul might term "petty politics": "You can't be released for more solitude because we need you to 'plug a hole." We need you to pull in a salary. It would be too much of a financial burden on the community." It is undeniably true that "man does not live by bread alone" (Mt 4:4), but neither does he live without some bread either (See Mk 6:30-44). In any case, God works through all these situations and at times in spite of them (see Is 55:8-11; Rm 8:28-39).

Thirdly, for as long as possible, the soul must continue forward on the same road that has brought it to where it is (Ph 3:16). It must continue to test honestly the authenticity of its own desire for more solitude, making every effort to listen with others to the ongoing revelation of God's will. It is possible that a call to greater solitude may be truly from God even though others cannot see it, for whatever reason. A director or a superior may not be able to see because of rigidity, fixed ideas, personality clash, closed-mindedness, stubbornness, etc. But God, for his own reasons, can simply withhold the gift of discernment from whomever he chooses, at whatever point that he wills in the discernment process. However, if the call is from God, the soul eventually reaches an inability to do other than follow it. That is, the soul reaches a point (a "crossroads," a "threshold") where it realizes that not to proceed in the direction of deeper exterior solitude would in fact do violence to its interior solitude. At this point the person must humbly follow his/her conscience and do whatever is necessary to ensure utmost fidelity to God's will whatever the cost.

We have attempted to present here sound principles and suggestions for the ongoing discernment in the case of a soul believing itself called by God to more intense physical solitude. Needless to say, the possible variations and nuances in the application of these principles to actual instances are myriad.

12

Contemplation and Asceticism

In its broadest sense, "ascetical" denotes that which the soul does or actively contributes towards its own sanctification following upon the initiative of God. On the other hand, "mystical" denotes that which God does or performs within the soul, the soul letting it be done.

In the process of spiritualization the mystical and ascetical elements blend into an ascending, spiral-like movement which evolves towards and converges upon transformation in Christ. Instead of the ascetical ceasing when the mystical begins, both the mystical and the ascetical elements are continuously interacting throughout the entirety of the process.

Even though the mystical element, which accentuates loving receptivity, is most pronounced in the wordless, imageless communing of contemplation, all forms of true prayer are nonetheless latent with a mystical or contemplative inner thrust. All prayer (communal, discursive, etc.) by virtue of its inner dynamism tends towards the simplicity of loving surrender.

The term "asceticism" is often used in reference to the performance of particular acts of mortification or virtue: for example, fasting, doing good deeds, attempting to overcome a personal fault by positive means, performing some act to strengthen a virtue.

To be spiritually beneficial an ascetical act of this sort must be a free and loving response to an interior inspiration from God that such and such a practice is indeed what he wants. True asceticism evolves out of a person's receptivity to God. By spiritually exercising and disposing the soul towards a more mature use of the created, ascetical practices make it ever more receptive to God himself. Throughout one's life of prayer, there will always be positive acts that God indicates to be performed in order that he may detach us all the more. Without asceticism in this sense, the mystical element of one's prayer-life cannot flourish.

However, asceticism, when practiced on one's own initiative without the inner promptings of grace, becomes an obstacle to mystic prayer. The inclination to seek out ascetical practices of one's own choosing is often merely a disguised attempt to become one's own savior and to avoid the painful experience of one's absolute dependency on God. This kind of "asceticism" is none other than a way of building up illusory spiritual security by measuring progress in holiness by the amount of success in living up to predetermined, self-imposed practices. Fixation on successfully accomplishing ascetical feats can only result in a heart closed to the unpredictable ways of God — a heart trapped in spiritual mediocrity and complacency. Such is not life "in faith" (Ga 2:20), but the pharisaical life (Ga 3-4).

Furthermore, despite one's good intentions, it is spiritually hazardous to attempt on one's own initiative to purify oneself. Beyond the little self-knowledge we may possess, there lies the vast mysterious realm of our being which we are utterly incapable of penetrating. The pruning of each soul is strictly the Father's business (see Jn 15:1-2): everything is pruned at the right time and in the proper measure. In the parable of the darnel, the wheat farmer advised his servants not to take upon themselves the responsibility of weeding out their fields: "No, because when you weed out the darnel you might pull out the wheat with it" (Mt 13:29).

Even the ascetical acts we perform in free and loving response to God are in themselves extremely limited in their capacity to purify: "No matter how much an individual does through his own efforts he cannot actively purify himself to be disposed in the least degree for the divine union of the perfection of love. God must take over and purge him in that fire that is dark for him."[1] This "taking over" by God St. John of the Cross calls "purgative contemplation."[2]

"No matter how earnestly the beginner in all his actions

---

[1] *Night*, I, 3, 3. See *Cloud*, 12.

[2] *Contemplación purgativa* (e.g., *Night*, I, Decl.). See *idem*, I, 10, 6 and II, 4, 1. This is sometimes referred to as "the night of contemplation" or "the contemplative night."

and passions practices the mortification of self, he will never be able to do so entirely — far from it! — until God accomplishes it in him passively by means of the purgation of this night."[3] All truly salvific purification is passive.

In the night of contemplation God still indicates particular acts which he wants the soul to perform. Yet, asceticism in the contemplative night consists principally in a general undergoing of whatever befalls the soul as a consequence of God's transforming influence within it.[4]

In prayer, for example, we must patiently endure (*padecer*) the ever growing aridity and persevere regardless of how strongly we may be inclined to think that we are wasting time and making no progress.[5] We must undergo (*padecer*) the storms, the aimless wandering of the imagination, the lack of sensory consolation. The time will come when the soul must even suffer (*padecer*) the apparent absence of God.[6] We must allow ourselves to experience the humiliation and dread of sin living in us, to admit the truth and misery of our creatureliness, to be contrite and repentant for faults and weaknesses.[7]

Deep spiritual anxiety must also be endured. As God leads us from the realm of quantity and empirical certitude to the way of obscure faith, we have the impression that the ground is slipping from beneath our feet. We experience a sense of

[3]*Night*, I, 7, 5.

[4]See *Night*, II, 5, 1.

[5]See *Night*, I, 10, 4-5.

[6]See *Canticle*, 1, 1-22.

[7]See *CP*, pp. 96-111; *Cloud*, 43, 44, 69, 70.

losing all control and security. We are losing control, of course, because God is gradually and systematically removing our defenses, leaving our hearts open and vulnerable to his love. As surface security and defenses slip away, we are forced to risk confronting and penetrating the vast, frightening chasm within us — a venture which we very carefully had avoided and which of ourselves we would lack the strength to undertake. On taking this leap in faith, it seems that we are journeying ever deeper into a dark infinite abyss. And the deeper in we are drawn, the more solitary it becomes.[8]

In this state the soul is often assailed by doubts, fears and agonizing questioning. There is the increasing uncertainty, perplexity and ambivalence at not having proof that what is happening is in fact leading to union in love, rather than to possible destruction. In passive purification we experience ourselves as being turned inside out. The freedom and love of God which has lured us into this darkness calls for a reshaping of our whole mode of existence. Consequently, we question our self-identity, our commitments, our personal value system, the values of the Church and of society. At times it seems we are actually losing our faith. Most painful of all is the feeling of despair — doubting even the relevance and power of God whom we love so intensely.

This apparent loss of faith (as well as trials of hope and love) is a necessary condition through which the soul must pass in order to receive deeper life in Christ. While it is experiencing this purgation as "loss," God in fact is stripping it of all the trappings that it believes to be faith, hope and love.

God does not effect our purification all at once, in one fell

[8]See *DM*, pp. 76-80.

swoop. He takes a lifetime. Purgation is a slow, all-embracing process in which God's transforming love consumes in us even the most minute vestige of immaturity. Why does God not purge us entirely, all at once? Why does he drag out the purification over a lifetime? Only our Father knows precisely. But in general we can say that he cannot do it because we simply could not take it. Such a radical purgation could quite literally kill us. The human nervous system and psyche —our human constitution — just could not take it all, all at once.

In the course of our life, the love of God demands not only that we let go our individualistic ways, prejudices and inordinate attachments, but most of all it demands that we let go our very self and remain abandoned to him in love alone. It is only through undergoing the gradual and systematic "annihilation of self" — wherein we experience the death throes of being reduced to "nothing" (*nada*) — that the love of God can reach its perfection in us. Paradoxically, it is when we lose ourselves that we find our true self in God: "Anyone who wants to save his life will lose it. But anyone who loses his life, for my sake, will find it" (Mt 16:25).

13

The Fruits of Contemplation

Although it appears sometimes that the soul is losing all spiritual benefits (the ability to meditate, consolations, sense of security, etc.), the contemplative experience — being loved by God and remaining loving him in return — affords a profound interior awakening which bears indescribable spiritual fruit: "Whoever remains in me, with me in him bears fruit in plenty. . . . It is to the glory of my Father that you should bear much fruit" (Jn 15:5, 8).[1]

The first and principal effect of contemplation is the experience of God within oneself. This is the very core of contemplation: the fact that God himself from within the soul

[1]John of the Cross treats the benefits caused by purgative contemplation in *Night*, I, 12-13. See *CP*, pp. 96-116.

directly and immediately[2] communicates himself to it in love. And the second principal effect is like the first: namely, God communing with the soul in love elicits the soul's loving response causing it to commune with him.

These are the first effects of contemplation in the ontological order (the order of being), but not necessarily in the psychological order (the order of awareness of the soul).

The most noticeable effect of contemplation in the psychological order is a purgative one: the awareness of an ever more profound experience of self, of one's insurmountable misery, out of which arises a deeper consciousness of the experience of God within us. We come to love God indescribably more through becoming aware of ourselves as being loved by him — despite our miserable selves and through no merit of our own (see Eph 2:4-10; Rm 7:24). We come to know him through being intimately known by him. We come to realize that if we thirst for him, he thirsts for us infinitely more. And if we desire him, his desire to draw us to himself is infinitely greater: "Let me know myself, Lord; let me know you."[3]

As a beginner in prayer, the soul experiences itself and God principally by means of discursive meditation, examination of conscience, interpersonal relationships, activity and various psychological aids and techniques. In other words, self-knowledge as well as knowledge of God is acquired principally

---

[2]"Immediately" not in the temporal sense of "all at once," but rather in the causal sense of "not through any created medium."

[3]Augustine, *Soliloquies*, II (*PL* 32, 885). Note that Augustine does not speak of knowledge *about* self or God. He speaks rather of direct experience: "know self," "know God."

through the mediation of something created.

While we become somewhat aware of certain personal limitations through this acquired knowledge, the predominant characteristic of our experience prior to contemplation is a consciousness of possessing self — a self with latent gifts and possibilities to be explored and developed. We are continuously confronted with making choices and decisions that determine our own personal identity and the future direction of our lives. In our interaction with the created, all our energies and efforts are channeled primarily towards building up a strong self for God. All this "ability" is received from God. But at this initial phase of self-consciousness, we are far more aware of what we are doing than of what we are receiving in order to do.

However, the development of self cannot continue indefinitely in the direction of building up self, since this necessarily brings the soul in touch with its innate limitation — the need to be redeemed: "Having taken its fill of the universe and of its own self, the soul finds that it is possessed by an indescribable need to die to self and to leave its own self behind (and this is not through disappointment, but rather as a logical development of its own effort)."[4]

So begins the other phase of the soul's transformation in Christ:[5] the phase of purgative contemplation. Herein God

[4]P. Teilhard de Chardin, *Forma Christi* (1918), in *Writings in Time of War* (Harper, 1965), p. 261. See *The Priest* (1918), *idem*, p. 222.

[5]In *Forma Christi* (*idem*, pp. 259-264), Teilhard treats of the two phases of the growth of the soul in Christ: the phase of a certain immersion in the universe (getting involved in creation) and the phase of emergence or detachment from everything created. These are but two aspects of one

himself detaches the soul in such a way that immersing it in himself, he causes it to emerge out of itself. The previous phase was distinguished by productivity, effort and success: "I must increase in order that Christ may increase." The final phase, however, is dominated by Christ. While preserving in the soul all the treasures of its individuality, he divests it of its egocentrism and causes it to cry: "I must decrease so that he may" further "increase" (Jn 3:30).

"This is the hour of the specifically Christian operation . . . . It is a grievous hour for our lower nature, abandoned to those forces in the world that bring diminishment, but one full of peace for the man who has the light of faith and believes that he is being driven out of himself and that he is dying under the compelling power of a Communion."[6]

Although God continues throughout one's life to furnish self-knowledge and knowledge of himself through the mediation of creatures, from the beginning of contemplation onward experience of self and of God is received principally as the fruit of the soul's immediate and direct communing with the indwelling triune God.

A most important aspect of the contemplative experience of self is the realization that *our* self is not *our* possession or attainment. "My life" (*vita mea*) is not really "mine" (*mei*), but rather "to me" (*mihi*). Our life is God's gift of his life in us: "I live now, not I, but Christ lives in me" (Ga 2:20).

Out of the inner depths of one's being breaks forth a

and the same movement, like breathing in and breathing out or like the arsis and thesis of a musical measure.

[6]*Forma Christi, idem*, p. 261. See *DM*, pp. 89-90.

consciousness of the two kinds of forces that act upon the soul from within and from without: the "passivities of growth" and the "passivities of diminishment."[7]

The passivities of growth, which by their nature favor our development, include our infinite capacity to love and be loved; our desire for being and becoming; our ability to act, to produce, to succeed; our personal talents and strengths of character. The other formidable forces assailing the soul from within as well as from without are the passivities of diminishment which apparently obstruct "growth" and diminish us: physical and intellectual limitations, weaknesses of all kinds, illness, sin, death. By virtue of the paschal mystery these forces of diminishment are in fact the passivities most charged with potential for growth — growth in Christ: for the weakness of man is the strength of God (1 Co 1:18-31; 2 Co 12:7-10 and 13:4).

Before the tide of chance and circumstance which threatens to inundate us and sweep us along haphazardly, we realize that there is a stronger power imposing a positive direction on all. We profoundly experience that God's providence is operative within all, turning everything to good for those who love him (Rm 8:28), recapitulating all in himself (Col 1:15-20).

"Yes, O God, I believe it! And I believe it all the more willingly because it is not only a question of my being consoled, but of my being completed. It is you who are at the origin of the impulse, and at the end of that continuing pull which all my life long I can do no other than follow, or favor the first impulse and its developments. And it is you who vivify for me with your omnipresence...the myriad of

[7] DM, pp. 76-93.

influences of which I am the constant object. In the life which wells up in me and in the matter which sustains me, I find much more than your gifts. It is you yourself whom I find, you who make me participate in your being, you who mold me."[8]

But, "grant, when my hour comes, that I may recognize you under the species of every alien or hostile force that seems bent upon destroying or uprooting me . . . . In all these dark moments, O God, grant that I may understand that it is you . . . who are painfully parting the fibres of my being in order to penetrate to the very marrow of my substance and bear me away within yourself."[9]

Integral to the experience of being acted upon by God within and without is the experience of oneself as creature, intimately and infinitely loved by God.

Because we lack direct awareness of the depth of our weaknesses and because we often expect clear proof that we are becoming holy, the experience of our creatureliness (itself the fruit of contemplation) makes us sometimes fear that we have been abandoned by God and that we are going astray. While any sincere soul would quite normally assume that the proper result of contemplation should be the awareness of becoming more selfless, patient and loving, the soul quickly discovers itself poor in spirit: selfish, lustful, resentful — incapable (of itself) of faithful love.

Yet, the ever increasing experience of the depths of creatureliness opens our consciousness to the increasing awareness of being empowered in weakness by God's superabundant and

[8]*DM*, p. 78.

[9]*DM*, pp. 89-90.

gratuitous love: "My grace is sufficient for you. My power is at its best in weakness" (2 Co 12:9).

The more intensely we experience the truth of our poverty, the more fully we experience the depths of God's intimate and redeeming love. No longer does the soul have to labor at self-analysis or formal examination of conscience. In purgative contemplation the slightest refusal to love, the slightest immaturity in our response to God's fidelity is immediately and intuitively perceived from within oneself. It sticks out like a sore thumb and moves us to seek forgiveness.

The experience of God in oneself is the milieu in which God brings forth all the other blessings of the night of contemplation: for example, humility, obedience, peace, freedom of spirit.

Humility is essentially a walking in truth. In the experience of God within oneself, we realize that all that we have, all that we are, all that we are becoming is received from God. "What do you have that you have not received?" (1 Co 4:7). As we grow in humility, judgmental attitudes towards self, God and others — attitudes deriving from our own standards of perfection — are mellowed. We grow in patience with our personal weaknesses and in compassion towards others in their weakness, as well as in deeper trust in God and in greater dependence upon him alone.

Obedience is the loving surrender of our will to the will of the Beloved. It disposes us to follow him in dark faith wherever he may lead, even when it is along a way we would rather not go. Obedience becomes concretized by fidelity in undergoing all that he reveals as his will, from within ourselves as well as through all the particular circumstances and persons that providentially enter our lives.

In contemplation, inner *peace* is indescribably intensified. The true peace which "the world cannot give" (Jn 14:27) is pure gift and transcends everything perceptible. Contrary to what some think, the peace of Christ may be present not only when we feel peaceful, but also in the midst of intense struggle, pain and darkness. Paradoxically in many instances, the peace of Christ actually produces the inner struggle, for there can be no peaceful coexistence between God in us and sin in us: "I have come to cast fire upon the earth..." (Lk 12:49-53).

Especially in the beginning of contemplation, this deeper, inner peace often goes unnoticed because of our preoccupation with the struggle: "Since this peace is something spiritual and delicate, its fruit is quiet, delicate, solitary, satisfying, peaceful and far removed from all these other gratifications of beginners which are so palpable and sensory."[10] However, perseverance in the night brings forth an unmistakable and undeniable awareness of an inner peace that is deeper than the darkness, that is beyond the struggle.

Rather than allowing us to rest comfortably, the peace of Christ intensifies our restless searching for our Beloved. As peace increases, so also does the wounding, burning desire to be found totally in God.[11]

[10]*Night*, I, 9, 7.

[11]According to John of the Cross, God's incomparable love for the soul heals and pacifies the soul in a series of successive wounds, each one more painful, more intense and more interior than the preceding one: first, *herida* (a kind of superficial wound), then *llaga* (a more penetrating wound), and finally *cauterio* (the wound by fire: cauterization). See *Canticle*, 1-7; *Flame*, 1-4.

Finally, *freedom of spirit* increases as God's transforming love purifies the soul of every attachment.

An attachment is an immaturity in the soul's attitude towards a creature. It does not imply that there is anything necessarily wrong with the creature. The creature as such does not cause the attachment, for the problem lies within the soul itself. Therefore, the detachment (*desnudez*) which transpires in purgative contemplation is not a cutting off or a withdrawal from creation. It is a correction of the soul's inordinate desire towards the created. Detachment is the process wherein God teaches the soul to love rightly both himself and his creation.[12]

The freedom of spirit that emerges in us as we become detached has nothing directly to do with the presence or the absence of persons, situations or things in our lives. That is, we can be detached from something which we in fact have, and we can covet something which we have not. Freedom of spirit then is the ability to love as God himself loves and to choose always what he wills.

Our inner transformation results in a transformed attitude towards everyone and everything: "Even though this blessed night darkens the spirit, it does so only to impart light concerning all things. And even though it humbles a person and reveals his miseries, it does so only to exalt him. And even though it impoverishes him and empties him of all possessions and natural affection, it does so only that he may reach out divinely to the enjoyment of all earthly and heavenly things at the same time maintaining a general freedom of spirit in them all."[13]

[12] See *Ascent*, I, 3, 4.

[13] *Night*, II, 9, 1.

14

An Integrating Prayer-Life

The mystery of divine love — being loved by God and remaining loving him in return — is as consistent as God himself: "God is love, and anyone abiding in love abides in God and God abides in him" (1 Jn 4:16). Furthermore, the mystery of divine love permeates every aspect of reality.

Contemplation, being a direct and immediate participation in this mystery, shares the same basic qualities of loving: namely, unlimited consistency (abiding forever) and all-pervasiveness (attaining to the most minute details of concrete existence). Once the threshold of contemplation is crossed one speaks not only of prayer, but of a *prayer-life* — and even more precisely, of an *integrating* prayer-life. That is, the quality of one's prayer actually integrates the whole of one's life.

This is more than a question of integrating prayer with the rest of one's life; or of integrating prayer, work, study, recreation, etc. with each other; or even of having an integrated prayer-life (integration between communal prayer, liturgical prayer, private prayer, etc.). The phrase "an integrating prayer-life" means rather that contemplation — continuously being loved by God and loving him directly, immediately — is itself the very source and principle of integration regarding the entirety of one's life. Without prayer in this sense, one's life can never become fully integrated.

There are in Scripture repeated exhortations calling us to maintain a consistent, all-pervasive attitude of prayer: "He told them a parable about the need to pray always..." (Lk 18:1). "Stay awake praying at all times..." (Lk 21:36). "Steadfastly continue in prayer..." (Rm 12:12). "Pray unceasingly ..." (1 Th 5:17). "Pray all the time ..." (Ep 6:18).

Let us consider three ingredients essential for allowing contemplation to integrate one's life: (1) solitude, (2) pondering the mysteries of salvation, (3) apostolate as prayer. These three elements assist also in intensifying the contemplative thrust already present in one's life.

(1) Solitude (Solitary Prayer):

The Gospel attests that Jesus consistently sought out solitude: "He would always go off to some place where he could be alone and pray" (Lk 5:16).

Consider the truth of this statement for a moment: "He

would always go off..." Jesus was forever doing this, constantly, habitually, repeatedly. "To some place where he could be alone..." That is, to an uninhabited, empty, deserted, solitary place — away from even his closest associates. "And pray" — he communed in kenosis with the Father and the Holy Spirit.

The sincere follower of Christ cannot but do the same: namely, consistently, regularly steal away to some solitary spot and pray. Daily time alone with God must be sought out, secured and made a priority, if we honestly desire God to deepen our loving communion with him. Exterior solitude cannot of course be equated with interior solitude. Nevertheless, *some* exterior solitude is necessary if our inner attitude of listening to God is to be intensified.

Why should this be so? Let us take an analogy from conjugal love. A husband and wife truly in love are continuously loving each other every moment of every day, even though they may not always be thinking of each other. Whether together or absent from one another, their mutual love goes on. Love is constant, consistent, enduring. One does not turn love on and off. True love is everlasting. Yet, in order that the quality of conjugal love be sustained and deepened, it is necessary that a husband and wife set aside time to be alone together, free from all their usual preoccupations and concerns, simply remaining lovingly attentive one to the other. This time of "making love" is a time of unique intensity of the love that has been transpiring all along and which will continue to deepen as time goes on.

Similarly with regard to the love of God. Instead of being a break in the day from one's usual activity, solitary prayer is a most intense focusing of the soul upon the mystery which is continuously transpiring within itself as well as through all the concrete particulars of its life. To awaken more deeply the soul's consciousness to the mystery of its life in God and so enkindle further its loving communion with him, some exterior solitude is essential. While the loving communion between God and a soul is an ongoing consistent reality, the soul must take time daily to be alone with its Beloved, simply remaining lovingly attentive to him, listening to him in that attitude of "here-I-am." Unless a soul seriously seeks out God in solitude, the flame of its love soon begins to waver.

Frequently the question is asked: "How much solitary prayer is necessary?" The basic response to this question may be expressed thus: The length of time and the intensity of solitude required for a person's solitary prayer depend on what God wants from that individual at any given moment in his/her genesis in Christ. This is normally discerned on a day to day basis through one's vocation and in accordance with all the particulars of one's concrete life situation. For a person with community responsibilities who is involved in a full-time active ministry, one hour of solitary prayer a day may be considered a *practical minimum*. This would apply equally to a housewife or to a corporate executive. Usually, because of the many responsibilities and limitations of day to day living, one hour daily is a *practical maximum* as well. We say "minimum" or "maximum" in this sense: Do all that you can to secure an hour each day — an uninterrupted hour whenever possible. Then beyond the "hour," simply take advantage of the opportunities that Providence offers — five minutes here, ten minutes there — without counting the time.

This hour of solitary prayer should not be naively left until one feels like praying. Human beings quite naturally live and interact in a whole complex of structures, one of which is a daily schedule. A specific time is allotted for community functions, meals, ministry, leisure. It is only normal that prayer also be scheduled on a regular, consistent, daily basis.

Why an hour a day? God certainly does not need a full hour, but the soul does. One does not want to make a fetish out of the hour (any more than one would make a fetish out of any aspect of any schedule). Yet, a person truly experienced in solitary prayer intuitively realizes that on a regular basis an hour is the minimum span of time needed to pray in depth.

Whether we choose to pray early in the morning, during the course of the day, or late at night; whether we pray in our room, in a chapel or in some other solitary place — none of this, of itself, affects the quality of the prayer. Each person must discover the time and the place most conducive to loving communion with God dwelling within his/her innermost being.

Even when we have done our best to seek out an hour alone with God, interruptions may still occur: the telephone rings, an emergency arises, an unexpected visitor drops in. Jesus himself had to integrate similar situations: "He said to his apostles, 'You must come away to some desert place all by yourselves and rest for awhile'. . . . So they went off in a boat to a solitary place. . . . But the people saw them going, and many could guess where. So from every town they all hurried to the place on foot and reached it before them" (Mk 6:31-33).

When such demands are *from God* — and the supposition is that it is from God when the demand is reasonable — the soul, without becoming overly anxious or concerned, must exercise the flexibility and inner freedom necessary to let go the exterior solitude and abandon itself to God in and through the circumstance or person at hand. That is, the soul must address itself to the situation in freedom of spirit and with a listening heart. What may seem like an interruption to the soul is often God's way of leading it into deeper interior solitude. God uses such interruptions as a subtle test of the quality of one's solitude. They are not really "interruptions" at all. Rather they are "interventions" of God. The soul who experiences these as intrusions (i.e., as annoying, irritating) may well be in isolation rather than in solitude.

Note the ease and graciousness with which Jesus let go his exterior solitude when he discerned that it was the Father's will that he minister to the needy crowds: "As he stepped ashore he saw a large crowd, and he took pity on them because they were like sheep without a shepherd. And he set himself to teach them at some length" (Mk 6:34).

Another more problematic situation may arise when for an extended period — days, weeks, months — the authentic demands of one's apostolate make it impossible to find sufficient time and energy for even minimal solitary prayer. These "authentic demands" never endure indefinitely. Therefore, if the situation goes on and on, the soul must re-evaluate the whole complex of circumstances to re-discern what is truly from God and what is not. Moreover, we are not of course speaking of that kind of self-appointed busyness — even with spiritual works — which is but a disguised effort to try to escape God and the truth of oneself.

You may be confident that if you are unable to procure

sufficient solitude because of God-given responsibilities, sooner or later, one way or another, God himself will balance the books. In other words, if you are unable to seek out solitude, you can be sure that eventually solitude will seek you out — usually at a time and in a way that you would have least chosen or expected.

We must learn to recognize God's call to solitude in the ordinary daily events of life. In the height of apostolic activity, for example, a person may come down with the flu and be forced to rest in bed for days. Or, in traveling, one may find oneself stranded in an airport or in a bus terminal waiting for hours before it is possible to continue one's journey. Latent within such instances may well be a call by God to spend some unsought time alone with him in loving receptivity.

(2) Pondering the Mysteries of Salvation:

One sign of an authentic prayer-life is the presence within the soul of a delicate balance between loving receptivity and active searching. While the soul's loving receptivity is manifested in a most intense way in solitary prayer, the soul's spirit of searching becomes especially evident in its pondering the mysteries of salvation, after the example of Mary who "kept all these things, pondering them in her heart" (Lk 2:19).

An important means of pondering the mysteries of salvation, along with and integral to the traditional *lectio divina*, is the study of the Scriptures and of spirituality. This study, more experiential than academic in nature, is to be distinguished from random spiritual reading. Inconsistent, unorganized, cursory reading of spiritual authors may be nothing more than an unconscious escape from indepth searching or study.

Solitary prayer is a listening and loving attentiveness to God in faith. Study of the Scriptures and of spirituality is faith seeking understanding. By allowing ourselves to be challenged by each mystery of salvation, God not only dispels many illusions, but also intensifies our appreciation for the element of mystery in our spiritual life. He thus gifts us with deeper loving knowledge of himself, which is traditionally called "wisdom."

A particularly beneficial way to ponder the mysteries of salvation — provided a person has sufficient theological background — is to do a comprehensive study of the life and spiritual doctrine of a personally selected spiritual master: Jeremiah, John the Evangelist, Paul of Tarsus, Augustine, Gregory of Nyssa, Thomas Aquinas, Teresa of Jesus, John of the Cross, Therese of Lisieux, Teilhard de Chardin, John Henry Newman, Thomas Merton — just to mention a few.

This "sufficient theological background" need not necessarily be extensive academic course work. A theologically self-educated person may well qualify. And we must not forget that contemplation itself imparts a true theological wisdom to the soul, which is the most important prerequisite of all for such a study.

The criterion for selecting such a spiritual master would normally be that the soul is drawn *intuitively* to choose the particular author. The fact that a soul experiences an affinity towards a certain spiritual master usually indicates that certain aspects of the process of that author's transformation into the likeness of Christ are similar to the soul's own process of spiritualization. The study of such a master is then not only intellectual, but above all it is experiential — a veritable undergoing with another the experience of Christ. Through such an intense study the soul will be able to elicit very concrete principles of discernment relative to its own life in God.

How long might such an extensive undertaking last? Certainly years, maybe even decades. You can read in snatches, but in order to really study you need blocks of time in which to concentrate, analyze and synthesize. You need to make the time — of course, in accordance with all your other normal responsibilities — and stick to the study in a deeply disciplined and persevering fashion. Herein lies another inestimable benefit of such a project: namely, the very discipline and perseverance required to pursue something so intense and so prolonged.

Whether you choose to study the life and teachings of a spiritual master, or choose some other approach to the questions of pondering the mysteries of salvation, you must in any case allow yourself to be challenged deeply and constantly by persistent and regular study. Some may find time on a daily basis. Others may be able to set aside time only on a weekend or on a monthly basis. Whatever the manner, whatever the amount of time and frequency, study of Scripture and of spirituality is essential to an integrating prayer-life.

(3) Apostolate (or Ministry) as Prayer:

What we call today "apostolate" (or more frequently "ministry") St. Paul terms *charisma*: that is, a gift freely given to an individual by God for the benefit of others. The word "apostolate" itself is derived from the Greek verb *apostellein* ("to send forth"). Integral to the notion of apostolate is that of mission: being sent forth by God to others.

Jesus, reflecting on his mission, proclaims: "My food is to do the will of the One who sent me and to complete his work" (Jn 4:34). Jesus, being in intimate union with the Father, intuits the Father's will and surrenders in obedient submission. So one is this union of wills that in being sent forth Jesus himself does not even act in his own name, but uniquely at the behest of the Father: "The words I say to you, I do not say as from myself. It is the Father living in me who is doing this work" (Jn 14:10).

This truth is paramount if we are to appreciate the authentic notion and implementation of apostolate: namely, that one must not only be conscious of having been sent forth to accomplish the will of the Father, but also in the actual accomplishing of that will it is the Father himself who is doing his own work in and through the soul. Thus "my mission" is not really "mine," but "to me." It is the Father's work gratuitously entrusted to me in such a way that he is the One actually accomplishing it, while I simultaneously let it be done and do whatever it is that he wants me to do.

As with Jesus the soul's acceptance and actual fulfillment of its mission is a personal response to being sent forth by God. We minister to his people because we are sent by him to do so.

If we are sent to do the will of God, there must be discernment regarding our particular mission. This presupposes openness, listening and receptivity of heart not only at the outset but all the way through. God only gradually unfolds the many nuances contained within any particular apostolate: "The Lord Yahweh has given me a disciple's tongue. So that I may know how to reply to the wearied, he provides me with speech. Each morning he awakens me to listen, to listen like a disciple" (Is 50:4).

God has a single, unifying mission (call, vocation) for each individual person. That unique mission may, in the course of a lifetime, cut across several "vocations" or "apostolates" (as we might tend to categorize them). However, God's way is not at all our way, nor does his call within a soul have anything directly to do with our categories, plans or conceptualizations. We do not mean to imply that call, mission, activity, receptivity are all one and the same. Each notion says something that the other does not. Yet all these realities are intricately interrelated and at a certain depth they all converge upon the will of the Father — whatever he wills, however he wills it.

Thus, even our activity, that is, the specific "doing" of our mission — however meaningful or however banal we may experience it — comprises a contemplative thrust. It does so because the sending forth as well as the doing is initiated, directed and brought to completion by God. One does the will of the Father sometimes by *doing* something particular, something specific (which is what is generally understood by "activity"). And one sometimes does the will of the Father by *not doing* anything particular at all: just letting it be done (which is what is generally understood by "passivity"). In either case the will of the Father is done in and through the soul (even if oftentimes this is accomplished in spite of its ways, desires and categories).

By actually doing the will of the One who sent him, Jesus

helped to "complete his work" (Jn 4:34). Our activity in Christ unites us to his mission of continuing to complete the work of recapitulating all creation in himself (Col 1:15-20); of letting God become "all in all" (1 Co 15:28). Consequently, not only our intention to do God's will is important, but also the very activity itself is a positive contribution to the building up of the Kingdom: "Any increase I can bring upon myself or upon things is translated into some increase in my power to love and some progress in Christ's blessed hold upon the universe. Our work appears to us mainly as a way of earning our daily bread. But its essential virtue is on a higher level. Through it we complete in ourselves the subject of divine union. And through it again we somehow make grow in stature the divine term of the One with whom we are united, Our Lord Jesus Christ."[1]

Two very important conclusions flow from this theology of apostolate (mission, ministry): namely, (1) it is not really I who bring Christ to others. It is Christ who brings himself to others in and through me. And (2) this bringing of Christ by Christ to another is not as if grace were not already operative: that is, as if Christ were not already present in the person, in the situation and in the encounter prior to my coming into the picture. Thus my principal responsibility in the matter is to foster the circumstances necessary for a true awareness, a true consciousness of him who is already there within.

Therefore, not only am I sent forth by God to others, but at the same time those to whom I am sent are sent by God to me. They are sent to me to further awaken my consciousness to his life within me: "Whatever is done to us, it is Christ who

[1]DM, p. 63.

does it. Whatever we do, it is to Christ that we do it."[2]

Apostolate in the sense in which we have been presenting it is obviously integral to one's prayer-life. Apostolate is not merely "a prayer," it is actual praying. An authentic sense of mission requires constant disposability and listening to God. It requires loving receptivity to let him use me to awaken others to his indwelling. It postulates loving openness to receive him more fully through those to whom I am sent.

One's "being" in God and one's "mission" by God are both given simultaneously in the single act of individual existence. These are but two aspects of one and the same mystery of our life in him: "Before I formed you in the womb I knew you. Before you came to birth I consecrated you. I sent you forth . . ." (Jr 1:5).

Jesus speaks to those who have become consecrated[3] "for my sake and for the sake of the gospel" (Mk 10:29). They are the ones "living in faith, faith in the Son of God" (Ga 2:20). They commit that which is deepest and most mysterious in their own person to that which is deepest and most mysterious in the person of Jesus. They are the ones truly committed to building up the Kingdom by their whole being and ministry.

[2]This is a phrase which Teilhard puts into Latin: "*Quidquid patimur, Christum patimur. Quidquid agimus, Christus agitur*" (literally: "Whatever we suffer, we suffer Christ. Whatever we do, Christ is done.") See *Forma Christi* (1918), in *Writings in Time of War* (Harper, 1965), p. 259; DM, p. 123.

[3]We use the term "consecrated" here not necessarily in the restricted, canonical sense (e.g., in Holy Orders or formal Religious Profession), but rather in the more general sense of anyone conscious of having received a mission from God.

There is then no incompatibility between prayer and apostolate, or between a call to greater solitude and mission. The same interior stance of listening is necessary in both solitary prayer and ministry. Should a soul experience a dichotomy between prayer and apostolate, solitude and mission, the problem lies within the soul itself, in its own inability to integrate the intricacies of God's call: "There is no contradiction between action and contemplation when Christian apostolic activity is raised to the level of pure charity. On that level, action and contemplation are fused into one entity by the love of God and of our brother in Christ."[4]

P. Teilhard de Chardin expresses this same truth in other words: "Spiritual authors dispute whether activity should precede contemplation as a preparation, or whether it should flow from contemplation as a divine superabundance. I must confess that I do not understand such problems. Whether I am active or whether I am praying, whether I laboriously open my soul through work, or whether God assails my soul with passivities of growth or of diminishment — I am equally conscious in all instances of being united to Christ. . . . First, foremost and always I am in Christ Jesus. And only then do I act, or do I suffer, or do I contemplate."[5]

The absence of dichotomy and the absence of contradiction do not at all imply absence of tension. On the contrary, even in persons who have a profoundly integrated and integrating prayer-life a great deal of inner tension and struggle may still

[4]CP, p. 115. Merton goes on: "But the trouble is that if prayer is not itself deep, powerful and pure and filled at all times with the spirit of contemplation, Christian action can never really reach this high level."

[5]*My Universe* (1924), in *Science and Christ* (Collins, 1968), p. 75.

exist between the active and the contemplative dimensions of the daily living out of this integration.

A special problem which confronts the contemporary Christian is that of recognizing, in the face of the overwhelming needs of others, the fact that what God sends any of us to do is limited. Extending oneself beyond one's personal mission leads only to interior scatteredness. This is far removed from truly being about "the Father's business" (Lk 2:49). There are times when the soul must say "no" in order to say a deeper "yes."

Solitude, pondering the mysteries of salvation, apostolate as prayer: these are each fundamental means by which God interiorizes our contemplative attitude towards himself. These are the three principal pillars upon which an integrated and an integrating prayer-life rests. The interdependence of these pillars is such that if one begins to collapse, the others quickly follow suit. And conversely, for either solitary prayer, study or one's apostolate to attain its maximum potential of quality, the others must also receive diligent effort and attention.

Merton passes on this word of advice: "He who attempts to act and do things for others or for the world without deepening his own self-understanding, freedom and capacity to love, will have nothing to give others. He will communicate to them nothing but the contagion of his own obsessions, his aggressiveness, his ego-centered ambitions, his delusions about ends and means, his doctrinaire prejudices and ideas."[6]

In a balanced prayer-life, the manner in which solitude, study and apostolate are to be specifically integrated and harmonized requires continuous, painstaking discernment.

[6]*Contemplation in a World of Action* (Image, 1973), pp. 178-179.

Ultimately, it is God alone who interiorly recollects us and brings us to that wordless and solitary surrender of the heart which must characterize all facets of life. Yet, we must be ever watchful and alert, ready to do whatever he indicates is necessary in order that his will may be done in us and through us.

Conclusion

Contemplation as Ministry

Not only is authentic ministry prayer, but contemplation itself is ministry.

A great deal is being spoken today about ministerial (or apostolic) spirituality — even its contemplative dimension —but very little is said about contemplation itself being a true ministry within the Church. Let us, in conclusion then, offer a few insights into this aspect of contemplation.

Ministry within the Church

Ministry can be appreciated in depth only when it is viewed within the perspective of the mystery of the Church.

At the core of what the Church *does* is first and foremost what the Church *is*. And the Church is the sacrament of Christ: the extension into space and time of the integral mystery of Christ.

Inseparable from the mystery of the Church is its mission to love and to proclaim Christ within itself and to the world. This loving and this proclamation transpire in a special way through its various ministries.

Pope Paul VI in his apostolic letter *Ministries in the Church* teaches: "Even in the most ancient times certain ministries were established in the Church for the purpose of suitably giving worship to God and for offering service to the people of God."[1]

Thus, Pope Paul states the two fundamental purposes of ministry: worship of God and service to his people. An act of ministry may consist of either of these two distinct thrusts. Yet ministry in its deepest sense is always a blend of the two: a simple act of loving adoration through some particular service.

Contemplation is eminently loving adoration and it is spiritual service par excellence. Furthermore, contemplation is a radical participation in the solitary, desert, kenotic aspects of the mystery of Christ, of his people and of his Church.

Pauline Theology of Charisma

The scriptural basis of what we call today ministry is to a great extent found in St. Paul's theology of *charisma*. This Greek term denotes special spiritual gifts bestowed by God

[1]*Acta Apostolicae Sedis*, 64 (1972) 529.

upon individual Christians in view of service (ministry) to others.

St. Paul furnishes several lists of charisms. In Rm 12:6-8 he writes: "Our gifts (*charismata*) differ according to the grace (*charin*) given us: prophecy...administration, teaching, preaching, almsgiving, works of mercy." In Ep 4:12 Paul mentions others: apostles, evangelists, pastors — all "so that the saints together make a unity in the work of service, building up the Body of Christ."

However, the text in which Paul most thoroughly develops his theology of the *charismata* is 1 Co 12-14. He introduces the theme in 1 Co 12:4-5 by stressing their unity of origin and purpose: "There is a variety of *charismaton*, but always the same Spirit. There are all sorts of service to be done, but always the same Lord." Then Paul enumerates still other gifts: preaching with wisdom, preaching with instruction, healing, the power of miracles, discernment of spirits, tongues, the interpretation of tongues, etc.

In 1 Co 12:27-30 Paul lists in descending order the relative importance of the *charismata* which he has mentioned up to this point: "In the Church, God has given first place to apostles, the second to prophets, the third to teachers. After them miracles, and after them the gift of healing, helpers, good leaders, those with many languages..."

Finally, Paul concludes chapter 12 with a forceful statement challenging the Corinthians to go beyond *all* these: "Be ambitious for the higher gifts. For I am going to show you an even more excellent way..." (1 Co 12:31).

This "even more excellent way" is that of faith, hope and love, but "the greatest of these is love (*agape*)" (1 Co 13:13).

The Charism of Agape

If we examine the various contexts in which Paul uses *agape*, we find that he employs the term in reference to three basic aspects of the spiritual life: (1) God's love for us, (2) our love for God and (3) our love for one another. While these may appear at first glance as separate categories, in Paul's mind they are but different manifestations of one and the same reality: the love of God.

Agape in its deepest sense is the loving indwelling of God in each soul: that is, the Father loving the Son, the Son loving the Father, and both spirating in love the Holy Spirit. *Agape* is the soul loving God inasmuch as the Spirit interiorly enables it. *Agape* is God in one person loving God in another.

Whether *agape* refers to God's love for us, our love for him, or our love for one another, the same simple mystery transpires: God loving God in and through each person. And it is precisely this simplicity of love that Paul proclaims is the greatest of all *charismata*.

Contemplation as Agape

The most intense response of a person to this charism of love is contemplative prayer. Contemplating is loving!

Two New Testament affirmations of who/what God is are particularly revealing: "God is Spirit" (Jn 4:24); "God is Love" (1 Jn 4:16). God is Spirit in the fullest biblical sense of mysterious, transcendent, wholly other. God is Love in the richest scriptural sense of intimate, immanent, in-the-soul.

The underlying notion of *agape* is that the love of Father, Son and Spirit enflames and transforms creation in and through the soul. *Agape* is divine spiritual power at work within the universe and within each soul reconciling it and uniting it in Christ, "so that God may be all in all" (1 Co 15:28).

Contemplation is *agape* in its simplest and purest human form. Contemplation is none other than remaining loving one's Beloved according to the request of Jesus himself: "Remain in me, as I remain in you" (Jn 15:4).

Put very briefly then, contemplation is God's supreme gift (*charisma*) which enables the soul to love him beyond all words and all thoughts, beyond all specific acts, interior or exterior. It is just remaining loving God, and all creation in him, with the very love of God himself.

Contemplation as Ministry

This simple act of love which so characterizes contemplation is not just a private gift. The love of God, in its contemplative expression, not only transforms the individual soul, but in and through the soul, in a mysterious way, it also transforms the Church, the world.

The more faithful a person is to his/her call to this contemplative charism the greater and deeper will be his/her actual service to the People of God. "Service" not only in the sense of sharing the fruit of one's contemplation with others (which God may surely ask in particular instances), but *especially* in the sense that contemplation is *in itself* authentic ministry. Contemplation as love needs no reason for being outside itself — it needs no other purpose (other than love for the sake of Love). It does not have to be "in order that. . . ." It does not have to be destined directly "to. . ." or "for. . ." anything or anyone other than God in himself. Contemplation, like *agape*, contains eminently within itself its own reason for being. You love simply because you love Love.

Contemplation in itself is authentic charism (ministry, service) in the deepest biblical sense of the term: that which a person is given by God to be in such a way that Christ brings himself to others. Contemplation as the *charisma agape* is not so much the "service" of doing something; it is rather the supreme "ministry" of *being* in love with Love.

Sic finis libri, non autem finis quaerendi.

Select Bibliography

This is a select bibliography on contemplative prayer principally in the western Christian tradition. Some of the authors and works listed here were used directly in the preparation of this study, others were not. Some of these authors and works express theological views to which we do not subscribe. Yet, each contributes positively to a deeper understanding of the mystery of contemplation.

Bailey, Raymond, *Thomas Merton on Mysticism* (Doubleday, 1975).

von Balthasar, Hans Urs, *Prayer* (Paulist, 1967).

Baker, Augustin, *Holy Wisdom* (Christian Classics, 1972).

Bernard of Clairvaux, *On the Love of God* (Newman, 1951).

Bloom, Anthony, *Living Prayer* (Templegate, 1966).

Bonaventure, St., *The Goad of Divine Love* (Benziger, 1907).

Bouyer, Louis, *History of Christian Spirituality*, I, II, III (Seabury, 1963-1969).

Bro, Bernard, *Learning to Pray* (Alba, 1966).

Belorgey, Godefroid, *The Practice of Mental Prayer* (Newman, 1952).

de Caussade, Jean-Pierre, *Abandonment to Divine Providence* (Herder, 1921).

de Caussade, Jean-Pierre, *On Prayer* (Templegate, 1964).

Champion, Pierre, *The Spiritual Doctrine of Fr. Louis Lallemant* (Newman, 1955).

Chapman, John, *Spiritual Letters* (Christian Classics, 1935).

Dicken, E. W. Trueman, *The Crucible of Love* (Sheed, 1963).

Dionysius the Areopagite (Pseudo-), *Opera Omnia* (*PG*, 3,4).

Dubay, Thomas, *Pilgrims Pray* (Alba, 1974).

Diefenbach, Gabriel, *Common Mystic Prayer* (St. Anthony, 1947).

Garrigou-Lagrange, Reginald, *Christian Perfection and Contemplation* (Herder, 1958).

Graham, Aelred, *The Love of God* (Image, 1959).

Green, Thomas, *When the Well Runs Dry* (Ave Maria, 1978).

Guardini, Romano, *Prayer in Practice* (Pantheon, 1957).

de Guibert, Joseph, *Theology of the Spiritual Life* (Sheed, 1953).

Higgins, John, *Thomas Merton on Prayer* (Doubleday, 1971).

Hinnebusch, Paul, *Dynamic Contemplation* (Sheed, 1970).

Ignatius of Loyola, *Spiritual Exercises* (Image, 1964).

John of the Cross, *Complete Works* (trans. by Peers or Kavanaugh).

Johnston, William, *Mysticism of the Cloud of Unknowing* (Desclée, 1967).

Johnston, William, *Silent Music* (Collins, 1974).

Julian of Norwich, *Showings* (Paulist, 1978).

Leclercq, Jean, *Alone with God* (Farrar, 1961).

Leen, Edward, *Progress through Mental Prayer* (Sheed, 1935).

Maloney, George, *Inward Stillness* (Dimension, 1976).

Maloney, George, *The Breath of the Mystic* (Dimension, 1974).

Merton, Thomas, *Seeds of Contemplation* (New Directions, 1949).

Merton, Thomas, *New Seeds of Contemplation* (New Directions, 1961).

Merton, Thomas, *Disputed Questions* (Farrar, 1960).

Merton, Thomas, *Contemplation in a World of Action* (Doubleday, 1971).

Merton, Thomas, *Thoughts in Solitude* (Farrar, 1960).

Merton, Thomas, *Contemplative Prayer* (Herder, 1969).

Nemeck, Francis Kelly, *Receptivity* (Vantage Press, 516 W. 34th St., New York, NY 10001) 1984.

Poulain, Augustin, *The Graces of Interior Prayer* (Celtic Cross, 1978).

Pourrat, Pierre, *Christian Spirituality*, I, II, III, IV (Newman, 1953-1958).

Rahner, Karl, *Theological Investigations*, III, VII, VIII (Seabury, 1974-1977).

Stein, Edith, *The Science of the Cross* (Regnery, 1960).

Teilhard de Chardin, Pierre, *Divine Milieu* (Harper, 1960).

Teilhard de Chardin, Pierre, *Hymn of the Universe* (Harper, 1961).

Teilhard de Chardin, Pierre, *Writings in Time of War* (Harper, 1961).

Teresa of Jesus, *Complete Works* (trans. by Peers or Kavanaugh).

Underhill, Evelyn, *Mysticism* (Dutton, 1961).

Voillaume, Rene, *Faith and Contemplation* (Dimension, 1974).

_____ *The Art of Prayer* (Faber, 1976).

_____ *The Cloud of Unknowing* and *The Book of Privy Counseling* (Image, 1973).

_____ *Early Fathers from the Philokalia* (Faber, 1973).

_____ *Writings from the Philokalia on Prayer of the Heart* (Faber, 1975).

_____ *The Way of the Pilgrim* (Seabury, 1965).